The Theory of Spectra and Atomic Constitution

THREE ESSAYS

NIELS BOHR
PROFESSOR OF THEORETICAL PHYSICS IN
THE UNIVERSITY OF COPENHAGEN

HAWK PRESS

Published by

Hawk Press
4836/24, Ansari Road, Daryaganj
New Delhi - 110 002
Phones: +91-11-23278618, +91-11-43667199
E-mail: thehawkpress@gmail.com
www.thehawkpress.com

ISBN: 978-93-93971-25-8

PREFACE

THE three essays which here appear in English all deal with the application of the quantum theory to problems of atomic structure, and refer to the different stages in the development of this theory.

The first essay "On the spectrum of hydrogen" is a translation of a Danish address given before the Physical Society of Copenhagen on the 20th of December 1913, and printed in *Fysisk Tidsskrift*, XII. p. 97, 1914. Although this address was delivered at a time when the formal development of the quantum theory was only at its beginning, the reader will find the general trend of thought very similar to that expressed in the later addresses, which form the other two essays. As emphasized at several points the theory does not attempt an "explanation" in the usual sense of this word, but only the establishment of a connection between facts which in the present state of science are unexplained, that is to say the usual physical conceptions do not offer sufficient basis for a detailed description.

The second essay "On the series spectra of the elements" is a translation of a German address given before the Physical Society of Berlin on the 27th of April 1920, and printed in *Zeitschrift für Physik*, VI. p. 423, 1920. This address falls into two main parts. The considerations in the first part are closely related to the contents of the first essay; especially no use is made of the new formal conceptions established through the later development of the quantum theory. The second part contains a survey of the results reached by this development. An attempt is made to elucidate the problems by means of a general principle which postulates a formal correspondence between the fundamentally different conceptions of the classical electrodynamics and those of the quantum theory. The first germ of this correspondence principle may be found in the first essay in the deduction of the expression for the constant of the hydrogen spectrum in terms of Planck's constant and of the quantities which in Rutherford's atomic model are necessary for the description of the hydrogen atom.

The third essay "The structure of the atom and the physical and chemical properties of the elements" is based on a Danish address, given before a joint meeting of the Physical and Chemical Societies of Copenhagen on the 18th of October 1921, and printed in *Fysisk Tidsskrift*, XIX. p. 153, 1921. While the first two essays form verbal translations of the respective addresses, this essay differs from the Danish original in certain minor points. Besides the addition of a few new figures with explanatory text, certain passages dealing with problems discussed in the second essay are left out, and some remarks about recent contributions to the subject are inserted. Where such insertions have been introduced will clearly appear from the text. This essay is divided into four parts. The first two parts contain a survey of previous results concerning atomic problems and a short account of the theoretical ideas of the quantum theory. In the following parts it is shown how these ideas lead to a view of atomic constitution which seems to offer an explanation of the observed physical and chemical properties of the elements, and especially to bring the characteristic features of the periodic table into close connection with the interpretation of the optical and high frequency spectra of the elements.

For the convenience of the reader all three essays are subdivided into smaller paragraphs, each with a headline. Conforming to the character of the essays there is, however, no question of anything like a full account or even a proportionate treatment of the subject stated in these headlines, the principal object being to emphasize certain general views in a freer form than is usual in scientific treatises or text books. For the same reason no detailed references to the literature are given, although an attempt is made to mention the main contributions to the development of the subject. As regards further information the reader in the case of the second essay is referred to a larger treatise "On the quantum theory of line spectra," two parts of which have appeared in the Transactions of the Copenhagen Academy (*D. Kgl. Danske Vidensk. Selsk. Skrifter*, 8. Række, IV. 1, I and II, 1918),* where full references to the literature may be found. The proposed continuation of this treatise, mentioned at several places in the second essay, has for various reasons been delayed, but in the near future the work will be completed by the publication of a third part. It is my intention to deal more fully with the problems discussed in the third essay by a larger systematic

*See www.gutenberg.org/ebooks/47167.—*Trans.*

account of the application of the quantum theory to atomic problems, which is under preparation.

As mentioned both in the beginning and at the end of the third essay, the considerations which it contains are clearly still incomplete in character. This holds not only as regards the elaboration of details, but also as regards the development of the theoretical ideas. It may be useful once more to emphasize, that—although the word "explanation" has been used more liberally than for instance in the first essay—we are not concerned with a description of the phenomena, based on a well-defined physical picture. It may rather be said that hitherto every progress in the problem of atomic structure has tended to emphasize the well-known "mysteries" of the quantum theory more and more. I hope the exposition in these essays is sufficiently clear, nevertheless, to give the reader an impression of the peculiar charm which the study of atomic physics possesses just on this account.

I wish to express my best thanks to Dr A. D. Udden, University of Pennsylvania, who has undertaken the translation of the original addresses into English, and to Mr C. D. Ellis, Trinity College, Cambridge, who has looked through the manuscript and suggested many valuable improvements in the exposition of the subject.

N. BOHR.

COPENHAGEN,
May 1922.

CONTENTS

ESSAY I

ON THE SPECTRUM OF HYDROGEN

ESSAY II

ON THE SERIES SPECTRA OF THE ELEMENTS

ESSAY III

THE STRUCTURE OF THE ATOM AND THE PHYSICAL AND CHEMICAL PROPERTIES OF THE ELEMENTS

ESSAY I*

ON THE SPECTRUM OF HYDROGEN

Empirical spectral laws. Hydrogen possesses not only the smallest atomic weight of all the elements, but it also occupies a peculiar position both with regard to its physical and its chemical properties. One of the points where this becomes particularly apparent is the hydrogen line spectrum.

The spectrum of hydrogen observed in an ordinary Geissler tube consists of a series of lines, the strongest of which lies at the red end of the spectrum, while the others extend out into the ultra-violet, the distance between the various lines, as well as their intensities, constantly decreasing. In the ultra-violet the series converges to a limit.

Balmer, as we know, discovered (1885) that it was possible to represent the wave lengths of these lines very accurately by the simple law

$$\frac{1}{\lambda_n} = R\left(\frac{1}{4} - \frac{1}{n^2}\right), \tag{1}$$

where R is a constant and n is a whole number. The wave lengths of the five strongest hydrogen lines, corresponding to $n = 3, 4, 5, 6, 7$, measured in air at ordinary pressure and

*Address delivered before the Physical Society in Copenhagen, Dec. 20, 1913.

temperature, and the values of these wave lengths multiplied by $\left(\frac{1}{4}-\frac{1}{n^2}\right)$ are given in the following table:

n	$\lambda \cdot 10^8$	$\lambda \cdot \left(\frac{1}{4}-\frac{1}{n^2}\right) \cdot 10^{10}$
3	6563.04	91153.3
4	4861.49	91152.9
5	4340.66	91153.9
6	4101.85	91152.2
7	3970.25	91153.7

The table shows that the product is nearly constant, while the deviations are not greater than might be ascribed to experimental errors.

As you already know, Balmer's discovery of the law relating to the hydrogen spectrum led to the discovery of laws applying to the spectra of other elements. The most important work in this connection was done by Rydberg (1890) and Ritz (1908). Rydberg pointed out that the spectra of many elements contain series of lines whose wave lengths are given approximately by the formula

$$\frac{1}{\lambda_n} = A - \frac{R}{(n+\alpha)^2},$$

where A and α are constants having different values for the various series, while R is a universal constant equal to the constant in the spectrum of hydrogen. If the wave lengths are measured in vacuo Rydberg calculated the value of R to be 109675. In the spectra of many elements, as opposed to the simple spectrum of hydrogen, there are several series of lines whose wave lengths are to a close approximation given by Rydberg's formula if different values are assigned to the constants A and α. Rydberg showed, however, in his earliest work, that certain relations existed between the constants in the various series of the spectrum of one and the same element. These relations were later very successfully generalized by Ritz through the establishment of the "combination principle." According to this principle, the wave lengths of the various lines in the spectrum of an element may be expressed by the formula

$$\frac{1}{\lambda} = F_r(n_1) - F_s(n_2). \tag{2}$$

In this formula n_1 and n_2 are whole numbers, and $F_1(n)$, $F_2(n)$, ... is a series of functions of n, which may be written approximately

$$F_r(n) = \frac{R}{(n + \alpha_r)^2},$$

where R is Rydberg's universal constant and α_r is a constant which is different for the different functions. A particular spectral line will, according to this principle, correspond to each combination of n_1 and n_2, as well as to the functions $F_1, F_2, \ldots$. The establishment of this principle led therefore to the prediction of a great number of lines which were not included in the spectral formulae previously considered, and in a large number of cases the calculations were found to be in close agreement with the experimental observations. In the case of hydrogen Ritz assumed that formula (1) was a special case of the general formula

$$\frac{1}{\lambda} = R\left(\frac{1}{n_1^2} - \frac{1}{n_2^2}\right), \tag{3}$$

and therefore predicted among other things a series of lines in the infra-red given by the formula

$$\frac{1}{\lambda} = R\left(\frac{1}{9} - \frac{1}{n^2}\right).$$

In 1909 Paschen succeeded in observing the first two lines of this series corresponding to $n = 4$ and $n = 5$.

The part played by hydrogen in the development of our knowledge of the spectral laws is not solely due to its ordinary simple spectrum, but it can also be traced in other less direct ways. At a time when Rydberg's laws were still in want of further confirmation Pickering (1897) found in the spectrum of a star a series of lines whose wave lengths showed a very simple relation to the ordinary hydrogen spectrum, since to a very close approximation they could be expressed by the formula

$$\frac{1}{\lambda} = R\left(\frac{1}{4} - \frac{1}{(n+\frac{1}{2})^2}\right).$$

Rydberg considered these lines to represent a new series of lines in the spectrum of hydrogen, and predicted according to his theory the existence of still another series of hydrogen lines the wave lengths of which would be given by

$$\frac{1}{\lambda} = R\left(\frac{1}{(\frac{3}{2})^2} - \frac{1}{n^2}\right).$$

By examining earlier observations it was actually found that a line had been observed in the spectrum of certain stars which coincided closely with the first line in this series (corresponding to $n = 2$); from analogy with other spectra it was also to be expected that this would be the strongest line. This was regarded as a great triumph for Rydberg's theory and tended to remove all doubt that the new spectrum was actually due to hydrogen. Rydberg's view has therefore been generally accepted by physicists up to the present moment. Recently however the question has been reopened and Fowler (1912) has succeeded in observing the Pickering lines in ordinary laboratory experiments. We shall return to this question again later.

The discovery of these beautiful and simple laws concerning the line spectra of the elements has naturally resulted in many attempts at a theoretical explanation. Such attempts are very alluring because the simplicity of the spectral laws and the exceptional accuracy with which they apply appear to promise that the correct explanation will be very simple and will give valuable information about the properties of matter. I should like to consider some of these theories somewhat more closely, several of which are extremely interesting and have been developed with the greatest keenness and ingenuity, but unfortunately space does not permit me to do so here. I shall have to limit myself to the statement that not one of the theories so far proposed appears to offer a satisfactory or even a plausible way of explaining the laws of the line spectra. Considering our deficient knowledge of the laws which determine the processes inside atoms it is scarcely possible to give an explanation of the kind attempted in these theories. The inadequacy of our ordinary theoretical conceptions has become especially apparent from the important results which have been obtained in recent years from the theoretical and experimental study of the laws of temperature radiation. You will therefore understand that I shall not attempt to propose an explanation of the spectral laws; on the contrary I shall try to indicate a way in which it appears possible to bring the spectral laws into close connection with other properties of the elements, which appear to be equally inexplicable on the basis of the present state of the science. In these considerations I shall employ the results obtained from the study of temperature radiation as well as the view of atomic structure which has been reached by the study of the radioactive elements.

Laws of temperature radiation. I shall commence by mentioning the conclusions which have been drawn from experimental and theoretical work on temperature radiation.

Let us consider an enclosure surrounded by bodies which

are in temperature equilibrium. In this space there will be a certain amount of energy contained in the rays emitted by the surrounding substances and crossing each other in every direction. By making the assumption that the temperature equilibrium will not be disturbed by the mutual radiation of the various bodies Kirchhoff (1860) showed that the amount of energy per unit volume as well as the distribution of this energy among the various wave lengths is independent of the form and size of the space and of the nature of the surrounding bodies and depends only on the temperature. Kirchhoff's result has been confirmed by experiment, and the amount of energy and its distribution among the various wave lengths and the manner in which it depends on the temperature are now fairly well known from a great amount of experimental work; or, as it is usually expressed, we have a fairly accurate experimental knowledge of the "laws of temperature radiation."

Kirchhoff's considerations were only capable of predicting the existence of a law of temperature radiation, and many physicists have subsequently attempted to find a more thorough explanation of the experimental results. You will perceive that the electromagnetic theory of light together with the electron theory suggests a method of solving this problem. According to the electron theory of matter a body consists of a system of electrons. By making certain definite assumptions concerning the forces acting on the electrons it is possible to calculate their motion and consequently the energy radiated from the body per second in the form of electromagnetic oscillations of various wave lengths. In a similar manner the absorption of rays of a given wave length by a substance can be determined by calculating the effect of electromagnetic oscillations upon the motion of the electrons. Having investigated the emission and absorption of a body at all temperatures, and for rays of all wave lengths, it is possible, as Kirchhoff has shown, to determine immediately the laws of temperature radiation. Since the result is to be independent of the nature of the body we are justified in expecting an agreement with experiment, even though very special assumptions are made about the forces acting upon the electrons of the hypothetical substance. This naturally simplifies the problem considerably, but it is nevertheless sufficiently difficult and it is remarkable that it has been possible to make any advance at all in this direction. As is well known this has been done by Lorentz (1903). He calculated the emissive as well as the absorptive power of a metal for long wave lengths, using the same assumptions about the motions of the electrons in the metal that Drude (1900) employed in his calculation of the ratio of the electrical and thermal conductivities. Subsequently, by calculating the ratio of the emissive to the absorptive power, Lorentz really obtained an expression for the law of temperature radiation which for long wave lengths agrees remarkably well with experimental facts. In spite of this beautiful and promising result, it has nevertheless become apparent that the electromagnetic theory is incapable of explaining the law of temperature radiation. For, it is possible to show, that, if the investigation is not confined to oscillations of long wave lengths, as in Lorentz's work, but is also extended to oscillations corresponding to small wave lengths, results are obtained which are contrary to experiment. This is especially evident from Jeans' investigations (1905) in which he employed a very interesting statistical method first proposed by Lord Rayleigh.

We are therefore compelled to assume, that the classical electrodynamics does not agree with reality, or expressed more carefully, that it cannot be employed in calculating the absorption and emission of radiation by atoms. Fortunately, the law of temperature radiation has also successfully indicated the direction in which the necessary changes in the electrodynamics are to be sought. Even before the appearance of the papers by Lorentz and Jeans, Planck (1900) had derived theoretically a formula for the black body radiation which was in good agreement with the results of experiment. Planck did not limit himself exclusively to the classical electrodynamics, but introduced the further assumption that a system of oscillating electrical particles (elementary resonators) will neither radiate nor absorb energy continuously, as required by the ordinary electrodynamics, but on the contrary will radiate and absorb discontinuously. The energy contained within the system at any moment is always equal to a whole multiple of the so-called quantum of energy the magnitude of which is equal to $h\nu$, where h is Planck's constant and ν is the frequency of oscillation of the system per second. In formal respects Planck's theory leaves much to be desired; in certain calculations the ordinary electrodynamics is used, while in others assumptions distinctly at variance with it are introduced without any attempt being made to show that it is possible to give a consistent explanation of the procedure used. Planck's theory would hardly have acquired general recognition merely on the ground of its agreement with experiments on black body radiation, but, as you know, the theory has also contributed quite remarkably to the elucidation of many different physical phenomena, such as specific heats, photoelectric effect, X-rays and the absorption of heat rays by gases. These explanations involve more than the qualitative assumption of a discontinuous transformation of energy, for with the aid of Planck's constant h it seems to be possible, at least approximately, to account for a great number of phenomena about which nothing could be said previously. It is therefore hardly too early to express the opinion that, whatever the final explanation will be, the discovery of "energy quanta" must be considered as one of the most important results arrived at in physics, and must be taken into consideration in investigations of the properties of atoms and particularly in connection with any explanation of the spectral laws in which such phenomena as the emission and absorption of electromagnetic radiation are concerned.

The nuclear theory of the atom. We shall now consider the second part of the foundation on which we shall build, namely the conclusions arrived at from experiments with the rays emitted by radioactive substances. I have previously here in the Physical Society had the opportunity of speaking of the scattering of α rays in passing through thin plates, and to mention how Rutherford (1911) has proposed a theory for the structure of the atom in order to explain the remarkable and unexpected results of these experiments. I shall, therefore, only remind you that the characteristic feature of Rutherford's theory is the assumption of the existence of a positively charged nucleus inside the atom. A number of electrons are supposed to revolve in closed orbits around the nucleus, the number of these electrons being sufficient to neutralize the positive charge of the nucleus. The dimensions of the nucleus are supposed to be very small in comparison with the dimensions of the orbits of the electrons, and almost the entire mass of the atom is supposed to be concentrated in the nucleus.

According to Rutherford's calculation the positive charge of the nucleus corresponds to a number of electrons equal to about half the atomic weight. This number coincides approximately with the number of the particular element in the periodic system and it is therefore natural to assume that the number of electrons in the atom is exactly equal to this number. This hypothesis, which was first stated by van den Broek (1912), opens the possibility of obtaining a simple explanation of the periodic system. This assumption is strongly confirmed by experiments on the elements of small atomic weight. In the first place, it is evident that according to Rutherford's theory the α particle is the same as the nucleus of a helium atom. Since the α particle has a double positive charge it follows immediately that a neutral helium atom contains two electrons. Further the concordant results obtained from calculations based on experiments as different as the diffuse scattering of X-rays and the decrease in velocity of α rays in passing through matter render the conclusion extremely likely that a hydrogen atom contains only a single electron. This agrees most beautifully with the fact that J. J. Thomson in his well-known experiments on rays of positive electricity has never observed a hydrogen atom with more than a single positive charge, while all other elements investigated may have several charges.

Let us now assume that a hydrogen atom simply consists of an electron revolving around a nucleus of equal and opposite charge, and of a mass which is very large in comparison with that of the electron. It is evident that this assumption may explain the peculiar position already referred to which hydrogen occupies among the elements, but it appears at the outset completely hopeless to attempt to explain anything at all of the special properties of hydrogen, still less its line spectrum, on the basis of considerations relating to such a simple system.

Let us assume for the sake of brevity that the mass of the nucleus is infinitely large in proportion to that of the electron, and that the velocity of the electron is very small in comparison with that of light. If we now temporarily disregard the energy radiation, which, according to the ordinary electrodynamics, will accompany the accelerated motion of the electron, the latter in accordance with Kepler's first law will describe an ellipse with the nucleus in one of the foci. Denoting the frequency of revolution by ω, and the major axis of the ellipse by $2a$ we find that

$$\omega^2 = \frac{2W^3}{\pi^2 e^4 m}, \quad 2a = \frac{e^2}{W}, \tag{4}$$

where e is the charge of the electron and m its mass, while W is the work which must be added to the system in order to remove the electron to an infinite distance from the nucleus.

These expressions are extremely simple and they show that the magnitude of the frequency of revolution as well as the length of the major axis depend only on W, and are independent of the eccentricity of the orbit. By varying W we may obtain all possible values for ω and $2a$. This condition shows, however, that it is not possible to employ the above formulae directly in calculating the orbit of the electron in a hydrogen atom. For this it will be necessary to assume that the orbit of the electron cannot take on all values, and in any event, the line spectrum clearly indicates that the oscillations of the electron cannot vary continuously between wide limits. The impossibility of making any progress with a simple system like the one considered here might have been foretold from a consideration of the dimensions involved; for with the aid of e and m alone it is impossible to obtain a quantity which can be interpreted as a diameter of an atom or as a frequency.

If we attempt to account for the radiation of energy in

the manner required by the ordinary electrodynamics it will only make matters worse. As a result of the radiation of energy W would continually increase, and the above expressions (4) show that at the same time the frequency of revolution of the system would increase, and the dimensions of the orbit decrease. This process would not stop until the particles had approached so closely to one another that they no longer attracted each other. The quantity of energy which would be radiated away before this happened would be very great. If we were to treat these particles as geometrical points this energy would be infinitely great, and with the dimensions of the electrons as calculated from their mass (about 10^{-13} cm.), and of the nucleus as calculated by Rutherford (about 10^{-12} cm.), this energy would be many times greater than the energy changes with which we are familiar in ordinary atomic processes.

It can be seen that it is impossible to employ Rutherford's atomic model so long as we confine ourselves exclusively to the ordinary electrodynamics. But this is nothing more than might have been expected. As I have mentioned we may consider it to be an established fact that it is impossible to obtain a satisfactory explanation of the experiments on temperature radiation with the aid of electrodynamics, no matter what atomic model be employed. The fact that the deficiencies of the atomic model we are considering stand out so plainly is therefore perhaps no serious drawback; even though the defects of other atomic models are much better concealed they must nevertheless be present and will be just as serious.

Quantum theory of spectra. Let us now try to overcome these difficulties by applying Planck's theory to the problem.

It is readily seen that there can be no question of a direct application of Planck's theory. This theory is concerned with the emission and absorption of energy in a system of electrical particles, which oscillate with a given frequency per second, dependent only on the nature of the system and independent of the amount of energy contained in the system. In a system consisting of an electron and a nucleus the period of oscillation corresponds to the period of revolution of the electron. But the formula (4) for ω shows that the frequency of revolution depends upon W, i.e. on the energy of the system. Still the fact that we cannot immediately apply Planck's theory to our problem is not as serious as it might seem to be, for in assuming Planck's theory we have manifestly acknowledged the inadequacy of the ordinary electrodynamics and have definitely parted with the coherent group of ideas on which the latter theory is based. In fact in taking such a step we cannot expect that all cases of disagreement between the theoretical conceptions hitherto employed and experiment will be removed by the use of Planck's assumption regarding the quantum of the energy momentarily present in an oscillating system. We stand here almost entirely on virgin ground, and upon introducing new assumptions we need only take care not to get into contradiction with experiment. Time will have to show to what extent this can be avoided; but the safest way is, of course, to make as few assumptions as possible.

With this in mind let us first examine the experiments on temperature radiation. The subject of direct observation is the distribution of radiant energy over oscillations of the various wave lengths. Even though we may assume that this energy comes from systems of oscillating particles, we know little or nothing about these systems. No one has ever seen a Planck's resonator, nor indeed even measured its frequency of oscillation; we can observe only the period of oscillation of the radiation which is emitted. It is therefore very convenient that it is possible to show that to obtain the laws of temperature radiation it is not necessary to make any assumptions about the systems which emit the radiation except that the amount of energy emitted each time shall be equal to $h\nu$, where h is Planck's constant and ν is the frequency of the radiation. Indeed, it is possible to derive Planck's law of radiation from this assumption alone, as shown by Debye, who employed a method which is a combination of that of Planck and of Jeans. Before considering any further the nature of the oscillating systems let us see whether it is possible to bring this assumption about the emission of radiation into agreement with the spectral laws.

If the spectrum of some element contains a spectral line corresponding to the frequency ν it will be assumed that one of the atoms of the element (or some other elementary system) can emit an amount of energy $h\nu$. Denoting the energy of the atom before and after the emission of the radiation by E_1 and E_2 we have

$$h\nu = E_1 - E_2 \text{ or } \nu = \frac{E_1}{h} - \frac{E_2}{h}. \tag{5}$$

During the emission of the radiation the system may be regarded as passing from one state to another; in order to introduce a name for these states, we shall call them "stationary" states, simply indicating thereby that they form some kind of waiting places between which occurs the emission of the energy corresponding to the various spectral lines. As previously mentioned the spectrum of an element consists of a series of lines whose wave lengths may be expressed by the formula (2). By comparing this expression with the relation given above it is seen that—since $\nu = \frac{c}{\lambda}$, where c is the velocity of light—each of the spectral lines may be regarded as being emitted by the transition of a system between two stationary states in which the energy apart from an additive arbitrary constant is given by $-chF_r(n_1)$ and $-chF_s(n_2)$ respectively. Using this interpretation the combination principle asserts that a series of stationary states exists for the given system, and that it can pass from one to any other of these states with the emission of a monochromatic radiation. We see, therefore, that with a simple extension of our first assumption it is possible to give a formal explanation of the most general law of line spectra.

Hydrogen spectrum. This result encourages us to make an attempt to obtain a clear conception of the stationary states which have so far only been regarded as formal. With this end in view, we naturally turn to the spectrum of hydrogen. The formula applying to this spectrum is given by the expression

$$\frac{1}{\lambda} = \frac{R}{n_1^2} - \frac{R}{n_2^2}.$$

According to our assumption this spectrum is produced by transitions between a series of stationary states of a system, concerning which we can for the present only say that the energy of the system in the nth state, apart from an additive constant, is given by $-\frac{Rhc}{n^2}$. Let us now try to find a connection between this and the model of the hydrogen atom. We assume that in the calculation of the frequency of revolution of the electron in the stationary states of the atom it will be possible to employ the above formula for ω. It is quite natural to make this assumption; since, in trying to form a reasonable conception of the stationary states, there is, for the present at least, no other means available besides the ordinary mechanics.

Corresponding to the nth stationary state in formula (4) for ω, let us by way of experiment put $W = \frac{Rhc}{n^2}$. This gives us

$$\omega_n^2 = \frac{2}{\pi^2} \frac{R^3h^3c^3}{e^4mn^6}. \qquad (6)$$

The radiation of light corresponding to a particular spectral line is according to our assumption emitted by a transition between two stationary states, corresponding to two different frequencies of revolution, and we are not justified in expecting any simple relation between these frequencies of revolution of the electron and the frequency of the emitted radiation. You understand, of course, that I am by no means trying to give what might ordinarily be described as an explanation; nothing has been said here about how or why the radiation is emitted. On one point, however, we may expect a connection with the ordinary conceptions; namely, that it will be possible to calculate the emission of slow electromagnetic oscillations on the basis of the classical electrodynamics. This assumption is very strongly supported by the result of Lorentz's calculations which have already been described. From the formula for ω it is seen that the frequency of revolution decreases as n increases, and that the expression $\frac{\omega_n}{\omega_{n+1}}$ approaches the value 1.

According to what has been said above, the frequency of the radiation corresponding to the transition between the $(n+1)$th and the nth stationary state is given by

$$\nu = Rc\left(\frac{1}{n^2} - \frac{1}{(n+1)^2}\right).$$

If n is very large this expression is approximately equal to

$$\nu = 2Rc/n^3.$$

In order to obtain a connection with the ordinary electrodynamics let us now place this frequency equal to the frequency of revolution, that is

$$\omega_n = 2Rc/n^3.$$

Introducing this value of ω_n in (6) we see that n disappears from the equation, and further that the equation will be satisfied only if

$$R = \frac{2\pi^2 e^4 m}{ch^3}. \tag{7}$$

The constant R is very accurately known, and is, as I have said before, equal to 109675. By introducing the most recent values for e, m and h the expression on the right-hand side of the equation becomes equal to $1.09 \cdot 10^5$. The agreement is as good as could be expected, considering the uncertainty in the experimental determination of the constants e, m and h. The agreement between our calculations and the classical electrodynamics is, therefore, fully as good as we are justified in expecting.

We cannot expect to obtain a corresponding explanation of the frequency values of the other stationary states. Certain simple formal relations apply, however, to all the stationary states. By introducing the expression, which has been found for R, we get for the nth state $W_n = \frac{1}{2}nh\omega_n$. This equation is entirely analogous to Planck's assumption concerning the energy of a resonator. W in our system is readily shown to be equal to the average value of the kinetic energy of the electron during a single revolution. The energy of a resonator was shown by Planck you may remember to be always equal to $nh\nu$. Further the average value of the kinetic energy of Planck's resonator is equal to its potential energy, so that the average value of the kinetic energy of the resonator, according to Planck, is equal to $\frac{1}{2}nh\omega$. This analogy suggests another manner of presenting the theory, and it was just in this way that I was originally led into these considerations. When we consider how differently the equation is employed here and in Planck's theory it appears to me misleading to use this analogy as a foundation, and in the account I have given I have tried to free myself as much as possible from it.

Let us continue with the elucidation of the calculations, and in the expression for $2a$ introduce the value of W which corresponds to the nth stationary state. This gives us

$$2a = n^2 \cdot \frac{e^2}{chR} = n^2 \cdot \frac{h^2}{2\pi^2 me^2} = n^2 \cdot 1.1 \cdot 10^{-8}. \qquad (8)$$

It is seen that for small values of n, we obtain values for the major axis of the orbit of the electron which are of the same order of magnitude as the values of the diameters of the atoms calculated from the kinetic theory of gases. For large values of n, $2a$ becomes very large in proportion to the calculated dimensions of the atoms. This, however, does not necessarily disagree with experiment. Under ordinary circumstances a hydrogen atom will probably exist only in the state corresponding to $n = 1$. For this state W will have its greatest value and, consequently, the atom will have emitted the largest amount of energy possible; this will therefore represent the most stable state of the atom from which the system cannot be transferred except by adding energy to it from without. The large values for $2a$ corresponding to large n need not, therefore, be contrary to experiment; indeed, we may in these large values seek an explanation of the fact, that in the laboratory it has hitherto not been possible to observe the hydrogen lines corresponding to large values of n in Balmer's formula, while they have been observed in the spectra of certain stars. In order that the large orbits of the electrons may not be disturbed by electrical forces from the neighbouring atoms the pressure will have to be very low, so low, indeed, that it is impossible to obtain sufficient light from a Geissler tube of ordinary dimensions. In the stars, however, we may assume that we have to do with hydrogen which is exceedingly attenuated and distributed throughout an enormously large region of space.

The Pickering lines. You have probably noticed that we have not mentioned at all the spectrum found in certain stars which according to the opinion then current was assigned to hydrogen, and together with the ordinary hydrogen spectrum was considered by Rydberg to form a connected system of lines completely analogous to the spectra of other elements. You have probably also perceived that difficulties would arise in interpreting this spectrum by means of the assumptions which have been employed. If such an attempt were to be made it would be necessary to give up the simple considerations which lead to the expression (7) for the constant R. We shall see, however, that it appears possible to explain the occurrence of this spectrum in another way. Let us suppose that it is not due to hydrogen, but to some other simple system consisting of a single electron revolving about a nucleus with an electrical charge Ne. The expression for ω becomes then

$$\omega^2 = \frac{2}{\pi^2} \frac{W^3}{N^2 e^4 m}.$$

Repeating the same calculations as before only in the inverse order we find, that this system will emit a line spectrum given by the expression

$$\frac{1}{\lambda} = \frac{2\pi^2 N^2 e^4 m}{ch^3} \left(\frac{1}{n_1^2} - \frac{1}{n_2^2} \right) = R \left(\frac{1}{\left(\frac{n_1}{N}\right)^2} - \frac{1}{\left(\frac{n_2}{N}\right)^2} \right). \quad (9)$$

By comparing this formula with the formula for Pickering's and Rydberg's series, we see that the observed lines can be explained on the basis of the theory, if it be assumed that the spectrum is due to an electron revolving about a nucleus with a charge $2e$, or according to Rutherford's theory around the nucleus of a helium atom. The fact that the spectrum in question is not observed in an ordinary helium tube, but only in stars, may be accounted for by the high degree of ionization which is required for the production of this spectrum; a neutral helium atom contains of course two electrons while the system under consideration contains only one.

These conclusions appear to be supported by experiment. Fowler, as I have mentioned, has recently succeeded in observing Pickering's and Rydberg's lines in a laboratory experiment. By passing a very heavy current through a mixture of hydrogen and helium Fowler observed not only these lines but also a new series of lines. This new series was of the same general type, the wave length being given approximately by

$$\frac{1}{\lambda} = R\left(\frac{1}{(\frac{3}{2})^2} - \frac{1}{(n+\frac{1}{2})^2}\right).$$

Fowler interpreted all the observed lines as the hydrogen spectrum sought for. With the observation of the latter series of lines, however, the basis of the analogy between the hypothetical hydrogen spectrum and the other spectra disappeared, and thereby also the foundation upon which Rydberg had founded his conclusions; on the contrary it is seen, that the occurrence of the lines was exactly what was to be expected on our view.

In the following table the first column contains the wave lengths measured by Fowler, while the second contains the limiting values of the experimental errors given by him; in the third column we find the products of the wave lengths by the quantity $\left(\frac{1}{n_1^2} - \frac{1}{n_2^2}\right) \cdot 10^{10}$; the values employed for n_1 and n_2 are enclosed in parentheses in the last column.

The values of the products are seen to be very nearly equal, while the deviations are of the same order of magnitude as the limits of experimental error. The value of the

$\lambda \cdot 10^8$	Limit of error	$\lambda \cdot \left(\frac{1}{n_1^2} - \frac{1}{n_2^2}\right) \cdot 10^{10}$	
4685.98	0.01	22779.1	(3 : 4)
3203.30	0.05	22779.0	(3 : 5)
2733.34	0.05	22777.8	(3 : 6)
2511.31	0.05	22778.3	(3 : 7)
2385.47	0.05	22777.9	(3 : 8)
2306.20	0.10	22777.3	(3 : 9)
2252.88	0.10	22779.1	(3 : 10)
5410.5	1.0	22774	(4 : 7)
4541.3	0.25	22777	(4 : 9)
4200.3	0.5	22781	(4 : 11)

product

$$\lambda \left(\frac{1}{n_1^2} - \frac{1}{n_2^2}\right)$$

should for this spectrum, according to the formula (9), be exactly $\frac{1}{4}$ of the corresponding product for the hydrogen spectrum. From the tables on pages 2 and 25 we find for these products 91153 and 22779, and dividing the former by the latter we get 4.0016. This value is very nearly equal to 4; the deviation is, however, much greater than can be accounted for in any way by the errors of the experiments. It has been easy, however, to find a theoretical explanation of this point. In all the foregoing calculations we have assumed that the mass of the nucleus is infinitely great compared to that of the electron. This is of course not the case, even though it holds to a very close approximation; for a hydrogen atom the ratio of the mass of the nucleus to that of the electron will be about 1850 and for a helium atom four times as great.

If we consider a system consisting of an electron revolving about a nucleus with a charge Ne and a mass M, we find the following expression for the frequency of revolution of the system:

$$\omega^2 = \frac{2}{\pi^2}\,\frac{W^3(M+m)}{N^2e^4Mm}.$$

From this formula we find in a manner quite similar to that previously employed that the system will emit a line spectrum, the wave lengths of which are given by the formula

$$\frac{1}{\lambda} = \frac{2\pi^2N^2e^4mM}{ch^3(M+m)}\left(\frac{1}{n_1^2} - \frac{1}{n_2^2}\right). \tag{10}$$

If with the aid of this formula we try to find the ratio of the product for the hydrogen spectrum, to that of the hypothetical helium spectrum we get the value 4.00163 which is in complete agreement with the preceding value calculated from the experimental observations.

I must further mention that Evans has made some experiments to determine whether the spectrum in question is due to hydrogen or helium. He succeeded in observing one of the lines in very pure helium; there was, at any rate, not enough hydrogen present to enable the hydrogen lines to be observed. Since in any event Fowler does not seem to consider such evidence as conclusive it is to be hoped that these experiments will be continued. There is, however, also another possibility of deciding this question. As is evident from the formula (10), the helium spectrum under consideration should contain, besides the lines observed by Fowler, a series of lines lying close to the ordinary hydrogen lines. These lines may be obtained by putting $n_1 = 4$, $n_2 = 6, 8, 10$, etc. Even if these lines were present, it would be extremely difficult to observe them on account of their position with regard to the hydrogen lines, but should they be observed this would probably also settle the question of the origin of the spectrum, since no reason would seem to be left to assume the spectrum to be due to hydrogen.

Other spectra. For the spectra of other elements the problem becomes more complicated, since the atoms contain a larger number of electrons. It has not yet been possible on the basis of this theory to explain any other spectra besides those which I have already mentioned. On the other hand it ought to be mentioned that the general laws applying to the spectra are very simply interpreted on the basis of our assumptions. So far as the combination principle is concerned its explanation is obvious. In the method we have employed our point of departure was largely determined by this particular principle. But a simple explanation can be also given of the other general law, namely, the occurrence of Rydberg's constant in all spectral formulae. Let us assume that the spectra under consideration, like the spectrum of hydrogen, are emitted by a neutral system, and that they are produced by the binding of an electron previously removed from the system. If such an electron revolves about the nucleus in an orbit which is large in proportion to that of the other electrons it will be subjected to forces much the same as the electron in a hydrogen atom, since the inner electrons individually will approximately neutralize the effect of a part of the positive charge of the nucleus. We may therefore assume that for this system there will exist a series of stationary states in which the motion of the outermost electron is approximately the same as in the stationary states of a hydrogen atom. I shall not discuss these matters any further, but shall only mention that they lead to the conclusion that Rydberg's constant is not exactly the same for all elements. The expression for this constant will in fact contain the factor $\dfrac{M}{M+m}$, where M is the mass of the nucleus. The correction is exceedingly small for elements of large atomic weight, but for hydrogen it is, from the point of view of spectrum analysis, very considerable. If the procedure employed leads to correct results, it is not therefore permissible to calculate Rydberg's constant directly from the hydrogen spectrum; the value of the universal constant should according to the theory be 109735 and not 109675.

I shall not tire you any further with more details; I hope to return to these questions here in the Physical Society, and to show how, on the basis of the underlying ideas, it is possible to develop a theory for the structure of atoms and molecules. Before closing I only wish to say that I hope I have expressed myself sufficiently clearly so that you have appreciated the extent to which these considerations conflict with the admirably coherent group of conceptions which have been rightly termed the classical theory of electrodynamics. On the other hand, by emphasizing this conflict, I have tried to convey to you the impression that it may be also possible in the course of time to discover a certain coherence in the new ideas.

ESSAY II*

ON THE SERIES SPECTRA OF THE ELEMENTS

I. INTRODUCTION

The subject on which I have the honour to speak here, at the kind invitation of the Council of your society, is very extensive and it would be impossible in a single address to give a comprehensive survey of even the most important results obtained in the theory of spectra. In what follows I shall try merely to emphasize some points of view which seem to me important when considering the present state of the theory of spectra and the possibilities of its development in the near future. I regret in this connection not to have time to describe the history of the development of spectral theories, although this would be of interest for our purpose. No difficulty, however, in understanding this lecture need be experienced on this account, since the points of view underlying previous attempts to explain the spectra differ fundamentally from those upon which the following considerations rest. This difference exists both in the development of our ideas about the structure of the atom and in the manner in which these ideas are used in explaining the spectra.

We shall assume, according to Rutherford's theory, that an atom consists of a positively charged nucleus with a num-

---

*Address delivered before the Physical Society in Berlin, April 27, 1920.

ber of electrons revolving about it. Although the nucleus is assumed to be very small in proportion to the size of the whole atom, it will contain nearly the entire mass of the atom. I shall not state the reasons which led to the establishment of this nuclear theory of the atom, nor describe the very strong support which this theory has received from very different sources. I shall mention only that result which lends such charm and simplicity to the modern development of the atomic theory. I refer to the idea that the number of electrons in a neutral atom is exactly equal to the number, giving the position of the element in the periodic table, the so-called "atomic number." This assumption, which was first proposed by van den Broek, immediately suggests the possibility ultimately of deriving the explanation of the physical and chemical properties of the elements from their atomic numbers. If, however, an explanation of this kind is attempted on the basis of the classical laws of mechanics and electrodynamics, insurmountable difficulties are encountered. These difficulties become especially apparent when we consider the spectra of the elements. In fact, the difficulties are here so obvious that it would be a waste of time to discuss them in detail. It is evident that systems like the nuclear atom, if based upon the usual mechanical and electrodynamical conceptions, would not even possess sufficient stability to give a spectrum consisting of sharp lines.

In this lecture I shall use the ideas of the quantum theory. It will not be necessary, particularly here in Berlin, to consider in detail how Planck's fundamental work on temperature radiation has given rise to this theory, according to which the laws governing atomic processes exhibit a definite element of discontinuity. I shall mention only Planck's chief result about the properties of an exceedingly simple kind of atomic system, the Planck "oscillator." This consists of an electrically charged particle which can execute harmonic oscillations about its position of equilibrium with a frequency independent of the amplitude. By studying the statistical equilibrium of a number of such systems in a field of radiation Planck was led to the conclusion that the emission and absorption of radiation take place in such a manner, that, so far as a statistical equilibrium is concerned only certain distinctive states of the oscillator are to be taken into consideration. In these states the energy of the system is equal to a whole multiple of a so-called "energy quantum," which was found to be proportional to the frequency of the oscillator. The particular energy values are therefore given by the well-known formula

$$E_n = nh\omega, \tag{1}$$

where n is a whole number, ω the frequency of vibration of the oscillator, and h is Planck's constant.

If we attempt to use this result to explain the spectra of the elements, however, we encounter difficulties, because the motion of the particles in the atom, in spite of its simple structure, is in general exceedingly complicated compared with the motion of a Planck oscillator. The question then arises, how Planck's result ought to be generalized in order to make its application possible. Different points of view immediately suggest themselves. Thus we might regard this equation as a relation expressing certain characteristic properties of the distinctive motions of an atomic system and try to obtain the general form of these properties. On the other hand, we may also regard equation (1) as a statement about a property of the process of radiation and inquire into the general laws which control this process.

In Planck's theory it is taken for granted that the frequency of the radiation emitted and absorbed by the oscillator is equal to its own frequency, an assumption which may be written

$$\nu \equiv \omega, \tag{2}$$

if in order to make a sharp distinction between the frequency of the emitted radiation and the frequency of the particles in the atoms, we here and in the following denote the former by ν and the latter by ω. We see, therefore, that Planck's result may be interpreted to mean, that the oscillator can emit and absorb radiation only in "radiation quanta" of magnitude

$$\Delta E = h\nu. \tag{3}$$

It is well known that ideas of this kind led Einstein to a theory of the photoelectric effect. This is of great importance, since it represents the first instance in which the quantum theory was applied to a phenomenon of non-statistical character. I shall not here discuss the familiar difficulties to which the "hypothesis of light quanta" leads in connection with the phenomena of interference, for the explanation of which the classical theory of radiation has shown itself to be so remarkably suited. Above all I shall not consider the problem of the nature of radiation, I shall only attempt to show how it has been possible in a purely formal manner to develop a spectral theory, the essential elements of which may be considered as a simultaneous rational development of the two ways of interpreting Planck's result.

II. GENERAL PRINCIPLES OF THE QUANTUM THEORY OF SPECTRA

In order to explain the appearance of line spectra we are compelled to assume that the emission of radiation by an atomic system takes place in such a manner that it is not possible to follow the emission in detail by means of the usual conceptions. Indeed, these do not even offer us the means of calculating the frequency of the emitted radiation. We shall see, however, that it is possible to give a very simple explanation of the general empirical laws for the frequencies of the spectral lines, if for each emission of radiation by the atom we assume the fundamental law to hold, that during the entire period of the emission the radiation possesses one and the same frequency ν, connected with the total energy emitted by the *frequency relation*

$$h\nu = E' - E''. \tag{4}$$

Here E' and E'' represent the energy of the system before and after the emission.

If this law is assumed, the spectra do not give us information about the motion of the particles in the atom, as is supposed in the usual theory of radiation, but only a knowledge of the energy changes in the various processes which can occur in the atom. From this point of view the spectra show the existence of certain, definite energy values corresponding to certain distinctive states of the atoms. These states will be called the *stationary states* of the atoms, since we shall assume that the atom can remain a finite time in each state, and can leave this state only by a process of transition to another stationary state. Notwithstanding the fundamental departure from the ordinary mechanical and electrodynamical conceptions, we shall see, however, that it is possible to give a rational interpretation of the evidence provided by the spectra on the basis of these ideas.

Although we must assume that the ordinary mechanics cannot be used to describe the transitions between the stationary states, nevertheless, it has been found possible to develop a consistent theory on the assumption that the motion in these states can be described by the use of the ordinary mechanics. Moreover, although the process of radiation cannot be described on the basis of the ordinary theory of electrodynamics, according to which the nature of the radiation emitted by an atom is directly related to the harmonic components occurring in the motion of the system, there is found, nevertheless, to exist a far-reaching *correspondence* between the various types of possible transitions between the stationary states on the one hand and the various harmonic components of the motion on the other hand. This correspondence is of such a nature, that the present theory of spectra is in a certain sense to be regarded as a rational generalization of the ordinary theory of radiation.

Hydrogen spectrum. In order that the principal points may stand out as clearly as possible I shall, before considering the more complicated types of series spectra, first consider the simplest spectrum, namely, the series spectrum of hydrogen. This spectrum consists of a number of lines whose frequencies are given with great exactness by Balmer's formula

$$\nu = \frac{K}{(n'')^2} - \frac{K}{(n')^2}, \tag{5}$$

where K is a constant, and n' and n'' are whole numbers. If we put $n'' = 2$ and give to n' the values 3, 4, etc., we get the well-known Balmer series of hydrogen. If we put $n'' = 1$ or $n'' = 3$ we obtain respectively the ultra-violet and infrared series. We shall assume the hydrogen atom simply to consist of a positively charged nucleus with a single electron revolving about it. For the sake of simplicity we shall suppose the mass of the nucleus to be infinite in comparison with the mass of the electron, and further we shall disregard the small variations in the motion due to the change in mass of the electron with its velocity. With these simplifications the electron will describe a closed elliptical orbit with the nucleus at one of the foci. The frequency of revolution ω and the major axis $2a$ of the orbit will be connected with the energy of the system by the following equations:

$$\omega = \sqrt{\frac{2W^3}{\pi^2 e^4 m}}, \quad 2a = \frac{e^2}{W}. \tag{6}$$

Here e is the charge of the electron and m its mass, while W is the work required to remove the electron to infinity.

The simplicity of these formulae suggests the possibility of using them in an attempt to explain the spectrum of hydrogen. This, however, is not possible so long as we use the classical theory of radiation. It would not even be possible to understand how hydrogen could emit a spectrum consisting of sharp lines; for since ω varies with W, the frequency of the emitted radiation would vary continuously during the emission. We can avoid these difficulties if we use the ideas of the quantum theory. If for each line we form the product $h\nu$ by multiplying both sides of (5) by h, then, since the right-hand side of the resulting relation may be written as the difference of two simple expressions, we are led by comparison with formula (4) to the assumption that the separate lines of the spectrum will be emitted by transitions between two stationary states, forming members of an infinite series of states, in which the energy in the nth state apart from an arbitrary additive constant is determined by the expression

$$E_n = -\frac{Kh}{n^2}. \tag{7}$$

The negative sign has been chosen because the energy of the atom will be most simply characterized by the work W required to remove the electron completely from the atom. If we now substitute $\frac{Kh}{n^2}$ for W in formula (6), we obtain the following expression for the frequency and the major axis in the nth stationary state:

$$\omega_n = \frac{1}{n^3}\sqrt{\frac{2h^3K^3}{\pi^2 e^4 m}}, \quad 2a_n = \frac{n^2e^2}{hK}. \tag{8}$$

A comparison between the motions determined by these equations and the distinctive states of a Planck resonator may be shown to offer a theoretical determination of the constant K. Instead of doing this I shall show how the value of K can be found by a simple comparison of the spectrum emitted with the motion in the stationary states, a comparison which at the same time will lead us to the principle of correspondence.

We have assumed that each hydrogen line is the result of a transition between two stationary states of the atom corresponding to different values of n. Equations (8) show that the frequency of revolution and the major axis of the orbit can be entirely different in the two states, since, as the energy decreases, the major axis of the orbit becomes smaller and the frequency of revolution increases. In general, therefore, it will be impossible to obtain a relation between the frequency of revolution of the electrons and the frequency of the radiation as in the ordinary theory of radiation. If, however, we consider the ratio of the frequencies of revolution in two stationary states corresponding to given values of n' and n'', we see that this ratio approaches unity as n' and n'' gradually increase, if at the same time the difference $n' - n''$ remains unchanged. By considering transitions corresponding to large values of n' and n'' we may therefore hope to establish a certain connection with the ordinary theory. For the frequency of the radiation emitted by a transition, we get according to (5)

$$\nu = \frac{K}{(n'')^2} - \frac{K}{(n')^2} = (n' - n'')K\,\frac{n' + n''}{(n')^2(n'')^2}. \qquad (9)$$

If now the numbers n' and n'' are large in proportion to their difference, we see that by equations (8) this expression may be written approximately,

$$\nu \sim (n' - n'')\omega\sqrt{\frac{2\pi^2 e^4 m}{Kh^3}}, \qquad (10)$$

where ω represents the frequency of revolution in the one or the other of the two stationary states. Since $n' - n''$ is a whole number, we see that the first part of this expression, i.e. $(n' - n'')\omega$, is the same as the frequency of one of the harmonic components into which the elliptical motion may be decomposed. This involves the well-known result that for a system of particles having a periodic motion of frequency ω, the displacement ξ of the particles in a given direction in space may be represented as a function of the time by a trigonometric series of the form

$$\xi = \sum C_\tau \cos 2\pi(\tau\omega t + c_\tau), \tag{11}$$

where the summation is to be extended over all positive integral values of τ.

We see, therefore, that the frequency of the radiation emitted by a transition between two stationary states, for which the numbers n' and n'' are large in proportion to their difference, will coincide with the frequency of one of the components of the radiation, which according to the ordinary ideas of radiation would be expected from the motion of the atom in these states, provided the last factor on the right-hand side of equation (10) is equal to 1. This condition, which is identical to the condition

$$K = \frac{2\pi^2 e^4 m}{h^3}, \tag{12}$$

is in fact fulfilled, if we give to K its value as found from measurements on the hydrogen spectrum, and if for e, m and h we use the values obtained directly from experiment. This agreement clearly gives us a *connection between the spectrum and the atomic model of hydrogen*, which is as close as could reasonably be expected considering the fundamental difference between the ideas of the quantum theory and of the ordinary theory of radiation.

The correspondence principle. Let us now consider somewhat more closely this relation between the spectra one would expect on the basis of the quantum theory, and on the ordinary theory of radiation. The frequencies of the spectral lines calculated according to both methods agree completely in the region where the stationary states deviate only little from one another. We must not forget, however, that the mechanism of emission in both cases is different. The different frequencies corresponding to the various harmonic components of the motion are emitted simultaneously according to the ordinary theory of radiation and with a relative intensity depending directly upon the ratio of the amplitudes of these oscillations. But according to the quantum theory the various spectral lines are emitted by entirely distinct processes, consisting of transitions from one stationary state to various adjacent states, so that the radiation corresponding to the τth "harmonic" will be emitted by a transition for which $n' - n'' = \tau$. The relative intensity with which each particular line is emitted depends consequently upon the relative probability of the occurrence of the different transitions.

This correspondence between the frequencies determined by the two methods must have a deeper significance and we are led to anticipate that it will also apply to the intensities. This is equivalent to the statement that, when the quantum numbers are large, the relative probability of a particular transition is connected in a simple manner with the amplitude of the corresponding harmonic component in the motion.

This peculiar relation suggests a *general law for the oc-*

currence of transitions between stationary states. Thus we shall assume that even when the quantum numbers are small the possibility of transition between two stationary states is connected with the presence of a certain harmonic component in the motion of the system. If the numbers n' and n'' are not large in proportion to their difference, the numerical value of the amplitudes of these components in the two stationary states may be entirely different. We must be prepared to find, therefore, that the exact connection between the probability of a transition and the amplitude of the corresponding harmonic component in the motion is in general complicated like the connection between the frequency of the radiation and that of the component. From this point of view, for example, the green line H_β of the hydrogen spectrum which corresponds to a transition from the fourth to the second stationary state may be considered in a certain sense to be an "octave" of the red line H_α, corresponding to a transition from the third to the second state, even though the frequency of the first line is by no means twice as great as that of the latter. In fact, the transition giving rise to H_β may be regarded as due to the presence of a harmonic oscillation in the motion of the atom, which is an octave higher than the oscillation giving rise to the emission of H_α.

Before considering other spectra, where numerous opportunities will be found to use this point of view, I shall briefly mention an interesting application to the Planck oscillator. If from (1) and (4) we calculate the frequency, which would correspond to a transition between two particular states of such an oscillator, we find

$$\nu = (n' - n'')\omega, \tag{13}$$

where n' and n'' are the numbers characterizing the states. It was an essential assumption in Planck's theory that the frequency of the radiation emitted and absorbed by the oscillator is always equal to ω. We see that this assumption is equivalent to the assertion that transitions occur only between two successive stationary states in sharp contrast to the hydrogen atom. According to our view, however, this was exactly what might have been expected, for we must assume that the essential difference between the oscillator and the hydrogen atom is that the motion of the oscillator is simple harmonic. We can see that it is possible to develop a formal theory of radiation, in which the spectrum of hydrogen and the simple spectrum of a Planck oscillator appear completely analogous. This theory can only be formulated by one and the same condition for a system as simple as the oscillator. In general this condition breaks up into two parts, one concerning the fixation of the stationary states, and the other relating to the frequency of the radiation emitted by a transition between these states.

General spectral laws. Although the series spectra of the elements of higher atomic number have a more complicated structure than the hydrogen spectrum, simple laws have been discovered showing a remarkable analogy to the

Balmer formula. Rydberg and Ritz showed that the frequencies in the series spectra of many elements can be expressed by a formula of the type

$$\nu = f_{k''}(n'') - f_{k'}(n'), \tag{14}$$

where n' and n'' are two whole numbers and $f_{k'}$ and $f_{k''}$ are two functions belonging to a series of functions characteristic of the element. These functions vary in a simple manner with n and in particular converge to zero for increasing values of n. The various series of lines are obtained from this formula by allowing the first term $f_{k''}(n'')$ to remain constant, while a series of consecutive whole numbers are substituted for n' in the second term $f_{k'}(n')$. According to the Ritz *combination principle* the entire spectrum may then be obtained by forming every possible combination of two values among all the quantities $f_k(n)$.

The fact that the frequency of each line of the spectrum may be written as the difference of two simple expressions depending upon whole numbers suggests at once that the terms on the right-hand side multiplied by h may be placed equal to the energy in the various stationary states of the atom. The existence in the spectra of the other elements of a number of separate functions of n compels us to assume the presence not of one but of a number of series of stationary states, the energy of the nth state of the kth series apart from an arbitrary additive constant being given by

$$E_k(n) = -hf_k(n). \tag{15}$$

This complicated character of the ensemble of stationary states of atoms of higher atomic number is exactly what was to be expected from the relation between the spectra calculated on the quantum theory, and the decomposition of the motions of the atoms into harmonic oscillations. From this point of view we may regard the simple character of the stationary states of the hydrogen atom as intimately connected with the simple periodic character of this atom. Where the neutral atom contains more than one electron, we find much more complicated motions with correspondingly complicated harmonic components. We must therefore expect a more complicated ensemble of stationary states, if we are still to have a corresponding relation between the motions in the atom and the spectrum. In the course of the lecture we shall trace this correspondence in detail, and we shall be led to a simple explanation of the apparent capriciousness in the occurrence of lines predicted by the combination principle.

The following figure gives a survey of the stationary states of the sodium atom deduced from the series terms.

The stationary states are represented by black dots whose distance from the vertical line a—a is proportional to the numerical value of the energy in the states. The arrows in the figure indicate the transitions giving those lines of the sodium spectrum which appear under the usual conditions of excitation. The arrangement of the states in horizontal rows corresponds to the ordinary arrangement of the "spectral terms" in the spectroscopic tables. Thus, the states in the first row (S) correspond to the variable term in the

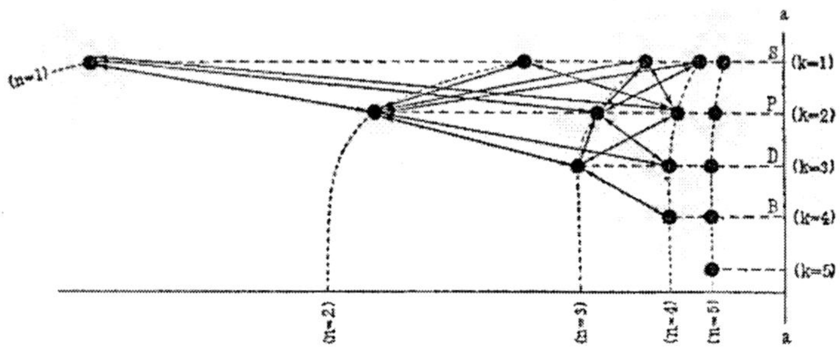

Diagram of the series spectrum of sodium.

"sharp series," the lines of which are emitted by transitions from these states to the first state in the second row. The states in the second row (P) correspond to the variable term in the "principal series" which is emitted by transitions from these states to the first state in the S row. The D states correspond to the variable term in the "diffuse series," which like the sharp series is emitted by transitions to the first state in the P row, and finally the B states correspond to the variable term in the "Bergmann" series (fundamental series), in which transitions take place to the first state in the D row. The manner in which the various rows are arranged with reference to one another will be used to illustrate the more detailed theory which will be discussed later. The apparent capriciousness of the combination principle, which I mentioned, consists in the fact that under the usual conditions of excitation not all the lines belonging to possible combinations of the terms of the sodium spectrum appear, but only those indicated in the figure by arrows.

The general question of the fixation of the stationary states of an atom containing several electrons presents difficulties of a profound character which are perhaps still far from completely solved. It is possible, however, to obtain an immediate insight into the stationary states involved in the emission of the series spectra by considering the empirical laws which have been discovered about the spectral terms. According to the well-known law discovered by Rydberg for the spectra of elements emitted under the usual conditions of excitation the functions $f_k(n)$ appearing in formula (14) can be written in the form

$$f_k(n) = \frac{K}{n^2}\phi_k(n), \tag{16}$$

where $\phi_k(n)$ represents a function which converges to unity for large values of n. K is the same constant which appears in formula (5) for the spectrum of hydrogen. This result must evidently be explained by supposing the atom to be electrically neutral in these states and one electron to be moving round the nucleus in an orbit the dimensions of which are very large in proportion to the distance of the other electrons from the nucleus. We see, indeed, that in this case the electric force acting on the outer electron will to a first approximation be the same as that acting upon the electron in the hydrogen atom, and the approximation will be the better the larger the orbit.

On account of the limited time I shall not discuss how

this explanation of the universal appearance of Rydberg's constant in the arc spectra is convincingly supported by the investigation of the "spark spectra." These are emitted by the elements under the influence of very strong electrical discharges, and come from ionized not neutral atoms. It is important, however, that I should indicate briefly how the fundamental ideas of the theory and the assumption that in the states corresponding to the spectra one electron moves in an orbit around the others, are both supported by investigations on selective absorption and the excitation of spectral lines by bombardment by electrons.

Absorption and excitation of radiation. Just as we have assumed that each emission of radiation is due to a transition from a stationary state of higher to one of lower energy, so also we must assume absorption of radiation by the atom to be due to a transition in the opposite direction. For an element to absorb light corresponding to a given line in its series spectrum, it is therefore necessary for the atom of this element to be in that one of the two states connected with the line possessing the smaller energy value. If we now consider an element whose atoms in the gaseous state do not combine into molecules, it will be necessary to assume that under ordinary conditions nearly all the atoms exist in that stationary state in which the value of the energy is a minimum. This state I shall call the *normal state*. We must therefore expect that the absorption spectrum of a monatomic gas will contain only those lines of the series spectrum, whose emission corresponds to transitions to the normal state. This expectation is completely confirmed by the spectra of the alkali metals. The absorption spectrum of sodium vapour, for example, exhibits lines corresponding only to the principal series, which as mentioned in the description of the figure corresponds with transitions to the state of minimum energy. Further confirmation of this view of the process of absorption is given by experiments on *resonance radiation.* Wood first showed that sodium vapour subjected to light corresponding to the first line of the principal series—the familiar yellow line—acquires the ability of again emitting a radiation consisting only of the light of this line. We can explain this by supposing the sodium atom to have been transferred from the normal state to the first state in the second row. The fact that the resonance radiation does not exhibit the same degree of polarization as the incident light is in perfect agreement with our assumption that the radiation from the excited vapour is not a resonance phenomenon in the sense of the ordinary theory of radiation, but on the contrary depends on a process which is not directly connected with the incident radiation.

The phenomenon of the resonance radiation of the yellow sodium line is, however, not quite so simple as I have indicated, since, as you know, this line is really a doublet. This means that the variable terms of the principal series are not simple but are represented by two values slightly different from one another. According to our picture of the origin of the sodium spectrum this means that the P states in the second row in the figure—as opposed to the S states in the first row—are not simple, but that for each place in this row there are two stationary states. The energy values differ so little from one another that it is impossible to represent them in the figure as separate dots. The emission (and absorption) of the two components of the yellow line are, therefore, connected with two different processes. This was beautifully shown by some later researches of Wood and Dunoyer. They found that if sodium vapour is subjected to radiation from only one of the two components of the yellow line, the resonance radiation, at least at low pressures, consists only of this component. These experiments were later continued by Strutt, and were extended to the case where the exciting line corresponded to the second line in the principal series. Strutt found that the resonance radiation consisted apparently only to a small extent of light of the same frequency as the incident light, while the greater part consisted of the familiar yellow line. This result must appear very astonishing on the ordinary ideas of resonance, since, as Strutt pointed out, no rational connection exists between the frequencies of the first and second lines of the principal series. It is however easily explained from our point of view. From the figure it can be seen that when an atom has been transferred into the second state in the second row, in addition to the direct return to the normal state, there are still two other transitions which may give rise to radiation, namely the transitions to the second state in the first row and to the first state in the third row. The experiments seem to indicate that the second of these three transitions is most probable, and I shall show later that there is some theoretical justification for this conclusion. By this transition, which results in the emission of an infra-red line which could not be observed with the experimental arrangement, the atom is taken to the second state of the first row, and from this state only one transition is possible, which again gives an infra-red line. This transition takes the atom to the first state in the second row, and the subsequent transition to the normal state then gives rise to the yellow line. Strutt discovered another equally surprising result, that this yellow resonance radiation seemed to consist of both components of the first line of the principal series, even when the incident light consisted of only one component of the second line of the principal series. This is in beautiful agreement with our picture of the phenomenon. We must remember that the states in the first row are simple, so when the atom has arrived in one of these it has lost every possibility of later giving any indication from which of the two states in the second row it originally came.

Sodium vapour, in addition to the absorption corresponding to the lines of the principal series, exhibits a *selective absorption in a continuous spectral region* beginning at the limit of this series and extending into the ultra-violet. This confirms in a striking manner our assumption that the absorption of the lines of the principal series of sodium results in final states of the atom in which one of the electrons revolves in larger and larger orbits. For we must assume that this continuous absorption corresponds to transitions from the normal state to states in which the electron is in a position to remove itself infinitely far from the nucleus. This phenomenon exhibits a complete analogy with the *photoelectric effect* from an illuminated metal plate in which, by using light of a suitable frequency, electrons of any velocity can be obtained. The frequency, however, must always lie above a certain limit connected according to Einstein's theory in a simple manner with the energy necessary to bring an electron out of the metal.

This view of the origin of the emission and absorption spectra has been confirmed in a very interesting manner by experiments on the *excitation of spectral lines and production of ionization by electron bombardment.* The chief advance in this field is due to the well-known experiments of Franck and Hertz. These investigators obtained their first important results from their experiments on mercury vapour, whose properties particularly facilitate such experiments. On account of the great importance of the results, these experiments have been extended to most gases and metals that can be obtained in a gaseous state. With the aid of the figure I shall briefly illustrate the results for the case of sodium vapour. It was found that the electrons upon colliding with the atoms were thrown back with undiminished velocity when their energy was less than that required to transfer the atom from the normal state to the next succeeding stationary state of higher energy value. In the case of sodium vapour this means from the first state in the first row to the first state in the second row. As soon, however, as the energy of the electron reaches this critical value, a new type of collision takes place, in which the electron loses all its kinetic energy, while at the same time the vapour is excited and emits a radiation corresponding to the yellow line. This is what would be expected, if by the collision the atom was transferred from the normal state to the first one in the second row. For some time it was uncertain to what extent this explanation was correct, since in the experiments on mercury vapour it was found that, together with the occurrence of non-elastic impacts, ions were always formed in the vapour. From our figure, however, we would expect ions to be produced only when the kinetic energy of the electrons is sufficiently great to bring the atom out of the normal state to the common limit of the states. Later experiments, especially by Davis and Goucher, have settled this point. It has been shown that ions can only be directly produced by collisions when the kinetic energy of the electrons corresponds to the limit of the series, and that the ionization found at first was an indirect effect arising from the photoelectric effect produced at the metal walls of the apparatus by the radiation arising from the return of the mercury atoms to the normal state. These experiments provide a direct and independent proof of the reality of the distinctive stationary states, whose existence we were led to infer from the series spectra. At the same time we get a striking impression of the insufficiency of the ordinary electrodynamical and mechanical conceptions for the description of atomic processes, not only as regards the emission of radiation but also in such phenomena as the collision of free electrons with atoms.

III. DEVELOPMENT OF THE QUANTUM THEORY OF SPECTRA

We see that it is possible by making use of a few simple ideas to obtain a certain insight into the origin of the series spectra. But when we attempt to penetrate more deeply, difficulties arise. In fact, for systems which are not simply periodic it is not possible to obtain sufficient information about the motions of these systems in the stationary states from the numerical values of the energy alone; more determining factors are required for the fixation of the motion. We meet the same difficulties when we try to explain in detail the characteristic effect of external forces upon the spectrum of hydrogen. A foundation for further advances in this field has been made in recent years through a development of the quantum theory, which allows a fixation of the stationary states not only in the case of simple periodic systems, but also for certain classes of non-periodic systems. These are the *conditionally periodic systems* whose equations of motion can be solved by a "separation of the variables." If generalized coordinates are used the description of the motion of these systems can be reduced to the consideration of a number of generalized "components of motion." Each of these corresponds to the change of only one of the coordinates and may therefore in a certain sense be regarded as "independent." The method for the fixation of the stationary states consists in fixing the motion of each of these components by a condition, which can be considered as a direct generalization of condition (1) for a Planck oscillator, so that the stationary states are in general characterized by as many whole numbers as the number of the degrees of freedom which the system possesses. A considerable number of physicists have taken part in this development of the quantum theory, including Planck himself. I also wish to mention the important contribution made by Ehrenfest to this subject on the limitations of the applicability of the laws of mechanics to atomic processes. The decisive advance in the application of the quantum theory to spectra, however, is due to Sommerfeld and his followers. However, I shall not further discuss the systematic form in which these authors have presented their results. In a paper which appeared some time ago in the Transactions of the Copenhagen Academy, I have shown that the spectra, calculated with the aid of this method for the fixation of the stationary states, exhibit a correspondence with the spectra which should correspond to the motion of the system similar to that which we have already considered in the case of hydrogen. With the aid of this general correspondence I shall try in the remainder of this lecture to show how it is possible to present the theory of series spectra and the effects produced by external fields of force upon these spectra in a form which may be considered as the natural generalization of the foregoing considerations.

This form appears to me to be especially suited for future work in the theory of spectra, since it allows of an immediate insight into problems for which the methods mentioned above fail on account of the complexity of the motions in the atom.

Effect of external forces on the hydrogen spectrum. We shall now proceed to investigate the effect of small perturbing forces upon the spectrum of the simple system consisting of a single electron revolving about a nucleus. For the sake of simplicity we shall for the moment disregard the variation of the mass of the electron with its velocity. The consideration of the small changes in the motion due to this variation has been of great importance in the development of Sommerfeld's theory which originated in the explanation of the *fine structure of the hydrogen lines.* This fine structure is due to the fact, that taking into account the variation of mass with velocity the orbit of the electron deviates a little from a simple ellipse and is no longer exactly periodic. This deviation from a Keplerian motion is, however, very small compared with the perturbations due to the presence of external forces, such as occur in experiments on the Zeeman and Stark effects. In atoms of higher atomic number it is also negligible compared with the disturbing effect of the inner electrons on the motion of the outer electron. The neglect of the change in mass will therefore have no important influence upon the explanation of the Zeeman and Stark effects, or upon the explanation of the difference between the hydrogen spectrum and the spectra of other elements.

We shall therefore as before consider the motion of the unperturbed hydrogen atom as simply periodic and inquire in the first place about the stationary states corresponding to this motion. The energy in these states will then be determined by expression (7) which was derived from the spectrum of hydrogen. The energy of the system being given, the major axis of the elliptical orbit of the electron and its frequency of revolution are also determined. Substituting in formulae (7) and (8) the expression for K given in (12), we obtain for the energy, major axis and frequency of revolution in the nth state of the unperturbed atom the expressions

$$\begin{gathered} E_n = -W_n = -\frac{1}{n^2}\frac{2\pi^2 e^4 m}{h^2}, \\ 2a_n = n^2\frac{h^2}{2\pi^2 e^2 m}, \qquad \omega_n = \frac{1}{n^3}\frac{4\pi^2 e^4 m}{h^3}. \end{gathered} \tag{17}$$

We must further assume that in the stationary states of the unperturbed system the form of the orbit is so far undetermined that the eccentricity can vary continuously. This is not only immediately indicated by the principle of correspondence,—since the frequency of revolution is determined only by the energy and not by the eccentricity,—but also by the fact that the presence of any small external forces will in general, in the course of time, produce a finite change in the position as well as in the eccentricity of the periodic orbit, while in the major axis it can produce only small changes proportional to the intensity of the perturbing forces.

In order to fix the stationary states of systems in the presence of a given conservative external field of force, we shall have to investigate, on the basis of the principle of correspondence, how these forces affect the decomposition of the motion into harmonic oscillations. Owing to the external forces the form and position of the orbit will vary continuously. In the general case these changes will be so complicated that it will not be possible to decompose the perturbed motion into discrete harmonic oscillations. In such a case we must expect that the perturbed system will not possess any sharply separated stationary states. Although each emission of radiation must be assumed to be monochromatic and to proceed according to the general frequency condition we shall therefore expect the final effect to be a broadening of the sharp spectral lines of the unperturbed system. In certain cases, however, the perturbations will be of such a regular character that the perturbed system can be decomposed into harmonic oscillations, although the ensemble of these oscillations will naturally be of a more complicated kind than in the unperturbed system. This happens, for example, when the variations of the orbit with respect to time are periodic. In this case harmonic oscillations will appear in the motion of the system the frequencies of which are equal to whole multiples of the period of the orbital perturbations, and in the spectrum to be expected on the basis of the ordinary theory of radiation we would expect components corresponding to these frequencies. According to the principle of correspondence we are therefore immediately led to the conclusion, that to each stationary state in the unperturbed system there corresponds a number of stationary states in the perturbed system in such a manner, that for a transition between two of these states a radiation is emitted, whose frequency stands in the same relationship to the periodic course of the variations in the orbit, as the spectrum of a simple periodic system does to its motion in the stationary states.

The Stark effect. An instructive example of the appearance of periodic perturbations is obtained when hydrogen is subjected to the effect of a homogeneous electric field. The eccentricity and the position of the orbit vary continuously under the influence of the field. During these changes, however, it is found that the centre of the orbit remains in a plane perpendicular to the direction of the electric force and that its motion in this plane is simply periodic. When the centre has returned to its starting point, the orbit will resume its original eccentricity and position, and from this moment the entire cycle of orbits will be repeated. In this case the determination of the energy of the stationary states of the disturbed system is extremely simple, since it is found that the period of the disturbance does not depend upon the original configuration of the orbits nor therefore upon the position of the plane in which the centre of the orbit moves, but only upon the major axis and the frequency of revolution. From a simple calculation it is found that the period a is given by the following formula

$$\sigma = \frac{3eF}{8\pi^2 ma\omega}, \tag{18}$$

where F is the intensity of the external electric field. From analogy with the fixation of the distinctive energy values of a Planck oscillator we must therefore expect that the energy difference between two different states, corresponding to the same stationary state of the unperturbed system, will simply be equal to a whole multiple of the product of h by the period σ of the perturbations. We are therefore immediately led to the following expression for the energy of the stationary states of the perturbed system,

$$E = E_n + kh\sigma, \tag{19}$$

where E_n depends only upon the number n characterizing the stationary state of the unperturbed system, while k is a new whole number which in this case may be either positive or negative. As we shall see below, consideration of the relation between the energy and the motion of the system shows that k must be numerically less than n, if, as before, we place the quantity E_n equal to the energy $-W_n$ of the nth stationary state of the undisturbed atom. Substituting the values of W_n, ω_n and a_n given by (17) in formula (19) we get

$$E = -\frac{1}{n^2}\frac{2\pi^2 e^4 m}{h^2} + nk\frac{3h^2 F}{8\pi^2 em}. \tag{20}$$

To find the effect of an electric field upon the lines of the hydrogen spectrum, we use the frequency condition (4) and obtain for the frequency ν of the radiation emitted by a transition between two stationary states defined by the numbers n', k' and n'', k''

$$\nu = \frac{2\pi^2 e^4 m}{h^3}\left(\frac{1}{(n'')^2} - \frac{1}{(n'')^2}\right) + \frac{3h \cdot F}{8\pi^2 em}(n'k' - n''k''). \quad (21)$$

It is well known that this formula provides a complete explanation of the Stark effect of the hydrogen lines. It corresponds exactly with the one obtained by a different method by Epstein and Schwarzschild. They used the fact that the hydrogen atom in a homogeneous electric field is a conditionally periodic system permitting a separation of variables by the use of parabolic coordinates. The stationary states were fixed by applying quantum conditions to each of these variables.

We shall now consider more closely the correspondence between the changes in the spectrum of hydrogen due to the presence of an electric field and the decomposition of the perturbed motion of the atom into its harmonic components. Instead of the simple decomposition into harmonic components corresponding to a simple Kepler motion, the displacement ξ of the electron in a given direction in space can be expressed in the present case by the formula

$$\xi = \sum C_{\tau,\kappa} \cos 2\pi\{t(\tau\omega + \kappa\sigma) + c_{\tau,\kappa}\}, \quad (22)$$

where ω is the average frequency of revolution in the perturbed orbit and σ is the period of the orbital perturbations, while $C_{\tau,\kappa}$ and $c_{\tau,\kappa}$ are constants. The summation is to be extended over all integral values for τ and κ.

If we now consider a transition between two stationary states characterized by certain numbers n', k' and n'', k'', we find that in the region where these numbers are large compared with their differences $n' - n''$ and $k' - k''$, the frequency of the spectral line which is emitted will be given approximately by the formula

$$\nu \sim (n' - n'')\omega + (k' - k'')\sigma. \tag{23}$$

We see, therefore, that we have obtained a relation between the spectrum and the motion of precisely the same character as in the simple case of the unperturbed hydrogen atom. We have here a similar correspondence between the harmonic component in the motion, corresponding to definite values for τ and κ in formula (22), and the transition between two stationary states for which $n' - n'' = \tau$ and $k' - k'' = \kappa$.

A number of interesting results can be obtained from this correspondence by considering the motion in more detail. Each harmonic component in expression (22) for which $\tau + \kappa$ is an even number corresponds to a linear oscillation parallel to the direction of the electric field, while each component for which $\tau + \kappa$ is odd corresponds to an elliptical oscillation perpendicular to this direction. The correspondence principle suggests at once that these facts are connected with the *characteristic polarization* observed in the

Stark effect. We would anticipate that a transition for which $(n' - n'') + (k' - k'')$ is even would give rise to a component with an electric vector parallel to the field, while a transition for which $(n' - n'') + (k' - k'')$ is odd would correspond to a component with an electric vector perpendicular to the field. These results have been fully confirmed by experiment and correspond to the empirical rule of polarization, which Epstein proposed in his first paper on the Stark effect.

The applications of the correspondence principle that have so far been described have been purely qualitative in character. It is possible however to obtain a quantitative estimate of the relative intensity of the various components of the Stark effect of hydrogen, by correlating the numerical values of the coefficients $C_{\tau,\kappa}$ in formula (22) with the probability of the corresponding transitions between the stationary states. This problem has been treated in detail by Kramers in a recently published dissertation. In this he gives a thorough discussion of the application of the correspondence principle to the question of the intensity of spectral lines.

The Zeeman effect. The problem of the effect of a homogeneous magnetic field upon the hydrogen lines may be treated in an entirely analogous manner. The effect on the motion of the hydrogen atom consists simply of the superposition of a uniform rotation upon the motion of the electron in the unperturbed atom. The axis of rotation is parallel with the direction of the magnetic force, while the frequency of revolution is given by the formula

$$\sigma = \frac{eH}{4\pi mc}, \tag{24}$$

where H is the intensity of the field and c the velocity of light.

Again we have a case where the perturbations are simply periodic and where the period of the perturbations is independent of the form and position of the orbit, and in the present case, even of the major axis. Similar considerations apply therefore as in the case of the Stark effect, and we must expect that the energy in the stationary states will again be given by formula (19), if we substitute for σ the value given in expression (24). This result is also in complete agreement with that obtained by Sommerfeld and Debye. The method they used involved the solution of the equations of motion by the method of the separation of the variables. The appropriate coordinates are polar ones about an axis parallel to the field.

If we try, however, to calculate directly the effect of the field by means of the frequency condition (4), we immediately meet with an apparent disagreement which for some time was regarded as a grave difficulty for the theory. As both Sommerfeld and Debye have pointed out, lines are not observed corresponding to every transition between the stationary states included in the formula. We overcome this difficulty, however, as soon as we apply the principle of correspondence. If we consider the harmonic components of the motion we obtain a simple explanation both of the non-occurrence of certain transitions and of the observed polarization. In the magnetic field each elliptic harmonic component having the frequency $\tau\omega$ splits up into three harmonic components owing to the uniform rotation of the orbit. Of these one is rectilinear with frequency $\tau\omega$ oscillating parallel to the magnetic field, and two are circular with frequencies $\tau\omega+\sigma$ and $\tau\omega-\sigma$ oscillating in opposite directions in a plane perpendicular to the direction of the field. Consequently the motion represented by formula (22) contains no components for which κ is numerically greater than 1, in contrast to the Stark effect, where components corresponding to all values of κ are present. Now formula (23) again applies for large values of n and k, and shows the asymptotic agreement between the frequency of the radiation and the frequency of a harmonic component in the motion. We arrive, therefore, at the conclusion that transitions for which k changes by more than unity cannot occur. The argument is similar to that by which transitions between two distinctive states of a Planck oscillator for which the values of n in (1) differ by more than unity are excluded. We must further conclude that the various possible transitions consist of two types. For the one type corresponding to the rectilinear component, k remains unchanged, and in the emitted radiation which possesses the same frequency ν_0 as the original hydrogen line, the electric vector will oscillate parallel with the field. For the second type, corresponding to the circular components, k will increase or decrease by unity, and the radiation viewed in the direction of the field will be circularly polarized and have frequencies $\nu_0 + \sigma$ and $\nu_0 - \sigma$ respectively. These results agree with those of the familiar Lorentz theory. The similarity in the two theories is remarkable, when we recall the fundamental difference between the ideas of the quantum theory and the ordinary theories of radiation.

Central perturbations. An illustration based on similar considerations which will throw light upon the spectra of other elements consists in finding the effect of a small perturbing field of force radially symmetrical with respect to the nucleus. In this case neither the form of the orbit nor the position of its plane will change with time, and the perturbing effect of the field will simply consist of a uniform rotation of the major axis of the orbit. The perturbations are periodic, so that we may assume that to each energy value of a stationary state of the unperturbed system there belongs a series of discrete energy values of the perturbed system, characterized by different values of a whole number k. The frequency σ of the perturbations is equal to the frequency of rotation of the major axis. For a given law of force for the perturbing field we find that σ depends both on the major axis and on the eccentricity. The change in the energy of the stationary states, therefore, will not be given by an expression as simple as the second term in formula (19), but will be a function of k, which is different for different fields.

It is possible, however, to characterize by one and the same condition the motion in the stationary states of a hydrogen atom which is perturbed by any central field. In order to show this we must consider more closely the fixation of the motion of a perturbed hydrogen atom.

In the stationary states of the unperturbed hydrogen atom only the major axis of the orbit is to be regarded as fixed, while the eccentricity may assume any value. Since the change in the energy of the atom due to the external field of force depends upon the form and position of its orbit, the fixation of the energy of the atom in the presence of such a field naturally involves a closer determination of the orbit of the perturbed system.

Consider, for the sake of illustration, the change in the hydrogen spectrum due to the presence of homogeneous electric and magnetic fields which was described by equation (19). It is found that this energy condition can be given a simple geometrical interpretation. In the case of an electric field the distance from the nucleus to the plane in which the centre of the orbit moves determines the change in the energy of the system due to the presence of the field. In the stationary states this distance is simply equal to $\frac{k}{n}$ times half the major axis of the orbit. In the case of a magnetic field it is found that the quantity which determines the change of energy of the system is the area of the projection of the orbit upon a plane perpendicular to the magnetic force. In the various stationary states this area is equal to

$\frac{k}{n}$ times the area of a circle whose radius is equal to half the major axis of the orbit. In the case of a perturbing central force the correspondence between the spectrum and the motion which is required by the quantum theory leads now to the simple condition that in the stationary states of the perturbed system the minor axis of the rotating orbit is simply equal to $\frac{k}{n}$ times the major axis. This condition was first derived by Sommerfeld from his general theory for the determination of the stationary states of a central motion. It is easily shown that this fixation of the value of the minor axis is equivalent to the statement that the parameter $2p$ of the elliptical orbit is given by an expression of exactly the same form as that which gives the major axis $2a$ in the unperturbed atom. The only difference from the expression for $2a_n$ in (17) is that n is replaced by k, so that the value of the parameter in the stationary states of the perturbed atom is given by

$$2p_k = k^2 \frac{h^2}{2\pi^2 e^2 m}. \tag{25}$$

The frequency of the radiation emitted by a transition between two stationary states determined in this way for which n' and n'' are large in proportion to their difference is given by an expression which is the same as that in equation (23), if in this case ω is the frequency of revolution of the electron in the slowly rotating orbit and σ represents the frequency of rotation of the major axis.

Before proceeding further, it might be of interest to note

that this fixation of the stationary states of the hydrogen atom perturbed by external electric and magnetic forces does not coincide in certain respects with the theories of Sommerfeld, Epstein and Debye. According to the theory of conditionally periodic systems the stationary states for a system of three degrees of freedom will in general be determined by three conditions, and therefore in these theories each state is characterized by three whole numbers. This would mean that the stationary states of the perturbed hydrogen atom corresponding to a certain stationary state of the unperturbed hydrogen atom, fixed by one condition, should be subject to two further conditions and should therefore be characterized by two new whole numbers in addition to the number n. But the perturbations of the Keplerian motion are simply periodic and the energy of the perturbed atom will therefore be fixed completely by one additional condition. The introduction of a second condition will add nothing further to the explanation of the phenomenon, since with the appearance of new perturbing forces, even if these are too small noticeably to affect the observed Zeeman and Stark effects, the forms of motion characterized by such a condition may be entirely changed. This is completely analogous to the fact that the hydrogen spectrum as it is usually observed is not noticeably affected by small forces, even when they are large enough to produce a great change in the form and position of the orbit of the electron.

Relativity effect on hydrogen lines. Before leaving the hydrogen spectrum I shall consider briefly the effect of the variation of the mass of the electron with its velocity. In the preceding sections I have described how external fields of force split up the hydrogen lines into several components, but it should be noticed that these results are only accurate when the perturbations are large in comparison with the small deviations from a pure Keplerian motion due to the variation of the mass of the electron with its velocity. When the variation of the mass is taken into account the motion of the unperturbed atom will not be exactly periodic. Instead we obtain a motion of precisely the same kind as that occurring in the hydrogen atom perturbed by a small central field. According to the correspondence principle an intimate connection is to be expected between the frequency of revolution of the major axis of the orbit and the difference of the frequencies of the fine structure components, and the stationary states will be those orbits whose parameters are given by expression (25). If we now consider the effect of external forces upon the fine structure components of the hydrogen lines it is necessary to keep in mind that this fixation of the stationary states only applies to the unperturbed hydrogen atom, and that, as mentioned, the orbits in these states are in general already strongly influenced by the presence of external forces, which are small compared with those with which we are concerned in experiments on the Stark and Zeeman effects. In general the presence of such forces will lead to a great complexity of perturbations, and the atom will no longer possess a group of sharply defined stationary states. The fine structure components of a given hydrogen line will therefore become diffuse and merged together. There are, however, several important cases where this does not happen on account of the simple character of the perturbations. The simplest example is a hydrogen atom perturbed by a central force acting from the nucleus. In this case it is evident that the motion of the system will retain its centrally symmetrical character, and that the perturbed motion will differ from the unperturbed motion only in that the frequency of rotation of the major axis will be different for different values of this axis and of the parameter. This point is of importance in the theory of the spectra of elements of higher atomic number, since, as we shall see, the effect of the forces originating from the inner electrons may to a first approximation be compared with that of a perturbing central field. We cannot therefore expect these spectra to exhibit a separate effect due to the variation of the mass of the electron of the same kind as that found in the case of the hydrogen lines. This variation will not give rise to a splitting up into separate components but only to small displacements in the position of the various lines.

We obtain still another simple example in which the hydrogen atom possesses sharp stationary states, although the change of mass of the electron is considered, if we take an atom subject to a homogeneous magnetic field. The effect of such a field will consist in the superposition of a rotation of the entire system about an axis through the nucleus and parallel with the magnetic force. It follows immediately from this result according to the principle of correspondence that each fine structure component must be expected to split up into a normal Zeeman effect (Lorentz triplet). The problem may also be solved by means of the theory of conditionally periodic systems, since the equations of motion in the presence of a magnetic field, even when the change in the mass is considered, will allow of a separation of the variables using polar coordinates in space. This has been pointed out by Sommerfeld and Debye.

A more complicated case arises when the atom is exposed to a homogeneous electric field which is not so strong that the effect due to the change in the mass may be neglected. In this case there is no system of coordinates by which the equations of motion can be solved by separation of the variables, and the problem, therefore, cannot be treated by the theory of the stationary states of conditionally periodic systems. A closer investigation of the perturbations, however, shows them to be of such a character that the motion of the electrons may be decomposed into a number of separate harmonic components. These fall into two groups for which the direction of oscillation is either parallel with or perpendicular to the field. According to the principle of correspondence, therefore, we must expect that also in this case in the presence of the field each hydrogen line will consist of a number of sharp, polarized components. In fact by means of the principles I have described, it is possible to give a unique fixation of the stationary states. The problem of the effect of a homogeneous electric field upon the fine structure components of the hydrogen lines has been treated in detail from this point of view by Kramers in a paper which will soon be published. In this paper it will be shown how it appears possible to predict in detail the manner in which the fine structure of the hydrogen lines gradually changes into the ordinary Stark effect as the electric intensity increases.

Theory of series spectra. Let us now turn our attention once more to the problem of the series spectra of elements of higher atomic number. The general appearance of the Rydberg constant in these spectra is to be explained by assuming that the atom is neutral and that one electron revolves in an orbit the dimensions of which are large in comparison with the distance of the inner electrons from the nucleus. In a certain sense, therefore, the motion of the outer electron may be compared with the motion of the electron of the hydrogen atom perturbed by external forces, and the appearance of the various series in the spectra of the other elements is from this point of view to be regarded as analogous to the splitting up of the hydrogen lines into components on account of such forces.

In his theory of the structure of series spectra of the type exhibited by the alkali metals, Sommerfeld has made the assumption that the orbit of the outer electron to a first approximation possesses the same character as that produced by a simple perturbing central field whose intensity diminishes rapidly with increasing distance from the nucleus. He fixed the motion of the external electron by means of his general theory for the fixation of the stationary states of a central motion. The application of this method depends on the possibility of separating the variables in the equations of motion. In this manner Sommerfeld was able to calculate a number of energy values which can be arranged in rows just like the empirical spectral terms shown in the diagram of the sodium spectrum (p. 46). The states grouped together by Sommerfeld in the separate rows are exactly those which were characterized by one and the same value of k in our investigation of the hydrogen atom perturbed by a central force. The states in the first row of the figure (row S) correspond to the value $k = 1$, those of the second row (P) correspond to $k = 2$, etc. The states corresponding to one and the same value of n are connected by dotted lines which are continued so that their vertical asymptotes correspond to the energy value of the stationary states of the hydrogen atom. The fact that for a constant n and increasing values of k the energy values approach the corresponding values for the unperturbed hydrogen atom is immediately evident from the theory since the outer electron, for large values of the parameter of its orbit, remains at a great distance from the inner system during the whole revolution. The orbit will become almost elliptical and the period of rotation of the major axis will be very large. It can be seen, therefore, that the effect of the inner system on the energy necessary to remove this electron from the atom must become less for increasing values of k.

These beautiful results suggest the possibility of finding laws of force for the perturbing central field which would account for the spectra observed. Although Sommerfeld in this way has in fact succeeded in deriving formulae for the spectral terms which vary with n for a constant k in agreement with Rydberg's formulae, it has not been possible to explain the simultaneous variation with both k and n in any actual case. This is not surprising, since it is to be anticipated that the effect of the inner electrons on the spectrum could not be accounted for in such a simple manner. Further consideration shows that it is necessary to consider not only the forces which originate from the inner electrons but also to consider the effect of the presence of the outer electron upon the motion of the inner electrons.

Before considering the series spectra of elements of low atomic number I shall point out how the occurrence or non-occurrence of certain transitions can be shown by the correspondence principle to furnish convincing evidence in favour of Sommerfeld's assumption about the orbit of the outer electron. For this purpose we must describe the motion of the outer electron in terms of its harmonic components. This is easily performed if we assume that the presence of the inner electrons simply produces a uniform rotation of the orbit of the outer electron in its plane. On account of this rotation, the frequency of which we will denote by σ, two circular rotations with the periods $\tau\omega + \sigma$ and $\tau\omega - \sigma$ will appear in the motion of the perturbed electron, instead of each of the harmonic elliptical components with a period $\tau\omega$ in the unperturbed motion. The decomposition of the perturbed motion into harmonic components consequently will again be represented by a formula of the type (22), in which only such terms appear for which κ is equal to $+1$ or -1. Since the frequency of the emitted radiation in the regions where n and k are large is again given by the asymptotic formula (23), we at once deduce from the correspondence principle that the only transitions which can take place are those for which the values of k differ by unity. A glance at the figure for the sodium spectrum shows that this agrees exactly with the experimental results. This fact is all the more remarkable, since in Sommerfeld's theory the arrangement of the energy values of the stationary states in rows has no special relation to the possibility of transition between these states.

Correspondence principle and conservation of angular momentum. Besides these results the correspondence principle suggests that the radiation emitted by the perturbed atom must exhibit circular polarization. On account of the indeterminateness of the plane of the orbit, however, this polarization cannot be directly observed. The assumption of such a polarization is a matter of particular interest for the theory of radiation emission. On account of the general correspondence between the spectrum of an atom and the decomposition of its motion into harmonic components, we are led to compare the radiation emitted during the transition between two stationary states with the radiation which would be emitted by a harmonically oscillating electron on the basis of the classical electrodynamics. In particular the radiation emitted according to the classical theory by an electron revolving in a circular orbit possesses an angular momentum and the energy ΔE and the angular momentum ΔP of the radiation emitted during a certain time are connected by the relation

$$\Delta E = 2\pi\omega \cdot \Delta P. \tag{26}$$

Here ω represents the frequency of revolution of the electron, and according to the classical theory this is equal to the frequency ν of the radiation. If we now assume that the total energy emitted is equal to $h\nu$ we obtain for the total angular momentum of the radiation

$$\Delta P = \frac{h}{2\pi}. \tag{27}$$

It is extremely interesting to note that this expression is equal to the change in the angular momentum which the atom suffers in a transition where k varies by unity. For in Sommerfeld's theory the general condition for the fixation of the stationary states of a central system, which in the special case of an approximately Keplerian motion is equivalent to the relation (25), asserts that the angular momentum of the system must be equal to a whole multiple of $\frac{h}{2\pi}$, a condition which may be written in our notation

$$P = k\frac{h}{2\pi}. \tag{28}$$

We see, therefore, that this condition has obtained direct support from a simple consideration of the conservation of angular momentum during the emission of the radiation. I wish to emphasize that this equation is to be regarded as a rational generalization of Planck's original statement about the distinctive states of a harmonic oscillator. It may be of interest to recall that the possible significance of the angular momentum in applications of the quantum theory to atomic processes was first pointed out by Nicholson on the basis of the fact that for a circular motion the angular momentum is simply proportional to the ratio of the kinetic energy to the frequency of revolution.

In a previous paper which I presented to the Copenhagen Academy I pointed out that these results confirm the conclusions obtained by the application of the correspondence principle to atomic systems possessing radial or axial symmetry. Rubinowicz has independently indicated the conclusions which may be obtained directly from a consideration of conservation of angular momentum during the radiation process. In this way he has obtained several of our results concerning the various types of possible transitions and the polarization of the emitted radiation. Even for systems possessing radial or axial symmetry, however, the conclusions which we can draw by means of the correspondence principle are of a more detailed character than can be obtained solely from a consideration of the conservation of angular momentum. For example, in the case of the hydrogen atom perturbed by a central force we can only conclude that k cannot change by more than unity, while the correspondence principle requires that k shall vary by unity for every possible transition and that its value cannot remain unchanged. Further, this principle enables us not only to exclude certain transitions as being impossible—and can from this point of view be considered as a "selection principle"—but it also enables us to draw conclusions about the relative probabilities of the various possible types of transitions from the values of the amplitudes of the harmonic components. In the present case, for example, the fact that the amplitudes of those circular components which rotate in the same sense as the electron are in general greater than the amplitudes of those which rotate in the opposite sense leads us to expect that lines corresponding to transitions for which k decreases by unity will in general possess greater intensity than lines during the emission of which k increases by unity. Simple considerations like this, however, apply only to spectral lines corresponding to transitions from one and the same stationary state. In other cases when we wish to estimate the relative intensities of two spectral lines it is clearly necessary to take into consideration the relative number of atoms which are present in each of the two stationary states from which the transitions start. While the intensity naturally cannot depend upon the number of atoms in the final state, it is to be noticed, however, that in estimating the probability of a transition between two stationary states it is necessary to consider the character of the motion in the final as well as in the initial state, since the values of the amplitudes of the components of oscillation of both states are to be regarded as decisive for the probability.

To show how this method can be applied I shall return for a moment to the problem which I mentioned in connection with Strutt's experiment on the resonance radiation of sodium vapour. This involved the discussion of the relative probability of the various possible transitions which can start from that state corresponding to the second term in the second row of the figure on p. 46. These were transitions to the first and second states in the first row and to the first state in the third row, and the results of experiment indicate, as we saw, that the probability is greatest for the second transitions. These transitions correspond to those harmonic components having frequencies $2\omega + \sigma$, $\omega + \sigma$ and σ, and it is seen that only for the second transition do the amplitudes of the corresponding harmonic component differ from zero in the initial as well as in the final state. [In the next essay the reader will find that the values of quantum number n assigned in fig. 1 to the various stationary states must be altered. While this correction in no way influences the other conclusions in this essay it involves that the reasoning in this passage cannot be maintained.]

I have shown how the correspondence between the spectrum of an element and the motion of the atom enables us to understand the limitations in the direct application of the combination principle in the prediction of spectral lines. The same ideas give an immediate explanation of the interesting discovery made in recent years by Stark and his collaborators, that certain *new series of combination lines* appear with considerable intensity when the radiating atoms are subject to a strong external electric field. This phenomenon is entirely analogous to the appearance of the so-called combination tones in acoustics. It is due to the fact that the perturbation of the motion will not only consist in an effect upon the components originally present, but in addition will give rise to new components. The frequencies of these new components may be $\tau\omega + \kappa\sigma$, where κ is different from ± 1. According to the correspondence principle we must therefore expect that the electric field will not only influence the lines appearing under ordinary circumstances, but that it will also render possible new types of transitions which give rise to the "new" combination lines observed. From an estimate of the amplitudes of the particular components in the initial and final states it has even been found possible to account for the varying facility with which the new lines are brought up by the external field.

The general problem of the effect of an electric field on the spectra of elements of higher atomic number differs essentially from the simple Stark effect of the hydrogen lines, since we are here concerned not with the perturbation of a purely periodic system, but with the effect of the field on a periodic motion already subject to a perturbation. The problem to a certain extent resembles the effect of a weak electric force on the fine structure components of the hydrogen atom. In much the same way the effect of an electric field upon the series spectra of the elements may be treated directly by investigating the perturbations of the external electron. A continuation of my paper in the Transactions of the Copenhagen Academy will soon appear in which I shall show how this method enables us to understand the interesting observations Stark and others have made in this field.

The spectra of helium and lithium. We see that it has been possible to obtain a certain general insight into the origin of the series spectra of a type like that of sodium. The difficulties encountered in an attempt to give a detailed explanation of the spectrum of a particular element, however, become very serious, even when we consider the spectrum of helium whose neutral atom contains only two electrons. The spectrum of this element has a simple structure in that it consists of single lines or at any rate of double lines whose components are very close together. We find, however, that the lines fall into two groups each of which can be described by a formula of the type (14). These are usually called the (ortho) helium and parhelium spectra. While the latter consists of simple lines, the former possesses narrow doublets. The discovery that helium, as opposed to the alkali metals, possesses two complete spectra of the Rydberg type which do not exhibit any mutual combinations was so surprising that at times there has been a tendency to believe that helium consisted of two elements. This way out of the difficulty is no longer open, since there is no room for another element in this region of the periodic system, or more correctly expressed, for an element possessing a new spectrum. The existence of the two spectra can, however, be traced back to the fact that in the stationary states corresponding to the series spectra we have to do with a system possessing only one inner electron and in consequence the motion of the inner system, in the absence of the outer electron, will be simply periodic and therefore easily perturbed by external forces.

In order to illustrate this point we shall have to consider more carefully the stationary states connected with the origin of a series spectrum. We must assume that in these states one electron revolves in an orbit outside the nucleus and the other electrons. We might now suppose that in general a number of different groups of such states might exist, each group corresponding to a different stationary state of the inner system considered by itself. Further consideration shows, however, that under the usual conditions of excitation those groups have by far the greatest probability for which the motion of the inner electrons corresponds to the "normal" state of the inner system, i.e. to that stationary state having the least energy. Further the energy required to transfer the inner system from its normal state to another stationary state is in general very large compared with the energy which is necessary to transfer an electron from the normal state of the neutral atom to a stationary orbit of greater dimensions. Lastly the inner system is in general capable of a permanent existence only in its normal state. Now, the configuration of an atomic system in its stationary states and also in the normal state will, in general, be completely determined. We may therefore expect that the inner system under the influence of the forces arising from the presence of the outer electron can in the course of time suffer only small changes. For this reason we must assume that the influence of the inner system upon the motion of the external electron will, in general, be of the same character as the perturbations produced by a constant external field upon the motion of the electron in the hydrogen atom. We must therefore expect a spectrum consisting of an ensemble of spectral terms, which in general form a connected group, even though in the absence of external perturbing forces not every combination actually occurs. The case of the helium spectrum, however, is quite different since here the inner system contains only one electron the motion of which in the absence of the external electron is simple periodic provided the small changes due to the variation in the mass of the electron with its velocity are neglected. For this reason the form of the orbit in the stationary states of the inner system considered by itself will not be determined. In other words, the stability of the orbit is so slight, even if the variation in the mass is taken into account, that small external forces are in a position to change the eccentricity in the course of time to a finite extent. In this case, therefore, it is possible to have several groups of stationary states, for which the energy of the inner system is approximately the same while the form of the orbit of the inner electron and its position relative to the motion of the other electrons are so essentially different, that no transitions between the states of different groups can occur even in the presence of external forces. It can be seen that these conclusions summarize the experimental observations on the helium spectra.

These considerations suggest an investigation of the nature of the perturbations in the orbit of the inner electron of the helium atom, due to the presence of the external electron. A discussion of the helium spectrum from this point of view has recently been given by Landé. The results of this work are of great interest particularly in the demonstration of the large back effect on the outer electron due to the perturbations of the inner orbit which themselves arise from the presence of the outer electron. Nevertheless, it can scarcely be regarded as a satisfactory explanation of the helium spectrum. Apart from the serious objections which may be raised against his calculation of the perturbations, difficulties arise if we try to apply the correspondence principle to Landé's results in order to account for the occurrence of two distinct spectra showing no mutual combinations. To explain this fact it seems necessary to base the discussion on a more thorough investigation of the mutual perturbations of the outer and the inner orbits. As a result of these perturbations both electrons move in such an extremely complicated way that the stationary states cannot be fixed by the methods developed for conditionally periodic systems. Dr Kramers and I have in the last few years been engaged in such an investigation, and in an address on atomic problems at the meeting of the Dutch Congress of Natural and Medical Sciences held in Leiden, April 1919, I gave a short communication of our results. For various reasons we have up to the present time been prevented from publishing, but in the very near future we hope to give an account of these results and of the light which they seem to throw upon the helium spectrum.

The problem presented by the spectra of elements of higher atomic number is simpler, since the inner system is better defined in its normal state. On the other hand the difficulty of the mechanical problem of course increases with the number of the particles in the atom. We obtain an example of this in the case of lithium with three electrons. The differences between the spectral terms of the lithium spectrum and the corresponding spectral terms of hydrogen are very small for the variable term of the principal series ($k = 2$) and for the diffuse series ($k = 3$), on the other hand it is very considerable for the variable term of the sharp series ($k = 1$). This is very different from what would be expected if it were possible to describe the effect of the inner electron by a central force varying in a simple manner with the distance. This must be because the parameter of the orbit of the outer electron in the stationary states corresponding to the terms of the sharp series is not much greater than the linear dimensions of the orbits of the inner electrons. According to the principle of correspondence the frequency of rotation of the major axis of the orbit of the outer electron is to be regarded as a measure of the deviation of the spectral terms from the corresponding hydrogen terms. In order to calculate this frequency it appears necessary to consider in detail the mutual effect of all three electrons, at all events for that part of the orbit where the outer electron is very close to the other two electrons. Even if we assumed that we were fully acquainted with the normal state of the inner system in the absence of the outer electron—which would be expected to be similar to the normal state of the neutral helium atom—the exact calculation of this mechanical problem would evidently form an exceedingly difficult task.

Complex structure of series lines. For the spectra of elements of still higher atomic number the mechanical problem which has to be solved in order to describe the motion in the stationary states becomes still more difficult. This is indicated by the extraordinarily complicated structure of many of the observed spectra. The fact that the series spectra of the alkali metals, which possess the simplest structure, consist of double lines whose separation increases with the atomic number, indicates that here we have to do with systems in which the motion of the outer electron possesses in general a somewhat more complicated character than that of a simple central motion. This gives rise to a more complicated ensemble of stationary states. It would, however, appear that in the sodium atom the major axis and the parameter of the stationary states corresponding to each pair of spectral terms are given approximately by formulae (17) and (25). This is indicated not only by the similar part played by the two states in the experiments on the resonance radiation of sodium vapour, but is also shown in a very instructive manner by the peculiar effect of magnetic fields on the doublets. For small fields each component splits up into a large number of sharp lines instead of into the normal Lorentz triplet. With increasing field strength Paschen and Back found that this *anomalous Zeeman effect* changed into the normal Lorentz triplet of a single line by a gradual fusion of the components.

This effect of a magnetic field upon the doublets of the alkali spectrum is of interest in showing the intimate relation of the components and confirms the reality of the simple explanation of the general structure of the spectra of the alkali metals. If we may again here rely upon the correspondence principle we have unambiguous evidence that the effect of a magnetic field on the motion of the electrons simply consists in the superposition of a uniform rotation with a frequency given by equation (24) as in the case of the hydrogen atom. For if this were the case the correspondence principle would indicate under all conditions a normal Zeeman effect for each component of the doublets. I want to emphasize that the difference between the simple effect of a magnetic field, which the theory predicts for the fine structure of components of the hydrogen lines, and the observed effect on the alkali doublets is in no way to be considered as a contradiction. The fine structure components are not analogous to the individual doublet components, but each single fine structure component corresponds to the ensemble of components (doublet, triplet) which makes up one of the series lines in Rydberg's scheme. The occurrence in strong fields of the effect observed by Paschen and Back must therefore be regarded as a strong support for the theoretical prediction of the effect of a magnetic field on the fine structure components of the hydrogen lines.

It does not appear necessary to assume the "anomalous" effect of small fields on the doublet components to be due to a failure of the ordinary electrodynamical laws for the description of the motion of the outer electron, but rather to be connected with an effect of the magnetic field on that intimate interaction between the motion of the inner and outer electrons which is responsible for the occurrence of the doublets. Such a view is probably not very different from the "coupling theory" by which Voigt was able to account formally for the details of the anomalous Zeeman effect. We might even expect it to be possible to construct a theory of these effects which would exhibit a formal analogy with the Voigt theory similar to that between the quantum theory of the normal Zeeman effect and the theory originally developed by Lorentz. Time unfortunately does not permit me to enter further into this interesting problem, so I must refer you to the continuation of my paper in the Transactions of the Copenhagen Academy, which will contain a general discussion of the origin of series spectra and of the effects of electric and magnetic fields.

IV. CONCLUSION

In this lecture I have purposely not considered the question of the structure of atoms and molecules although this is of course most intimately connected with the kind of spectral theory I have developed. We are encouraged to use results obtained from the spectra, since even the simple theory of the hydrogen spectrum gives a value for the major axis of the orbit of the electron in the normal state ($n = 1$) of the same order of magnitude as that derived from the kinetic theory of gases. In my first paper on the subject I attempted to sketch a theory of the structure of atoms and of molecules of chemical compounds. This theory was based on a simple generalization of the results for the stationary states of the hydrogen atom. In several respects the theory was supported by experiment, especially in the general way in which the properties of the elements change with increasing atomic number, shown most clearly by Moseley's results. I should like, however, to use this occasion to state, that in view of the recent development of the quantum theory, many of the special assumptions will certainly have to be changed in detail. This has become clear from various sides by the lack of agreement of the theory with experiment. It appears no longer possible to justify the assumption that in the normal states the electrons move in orbits of special geometrical simplicity, like "electronic rings." Considerations relating to the stability of atoms and molecules against external influences and concerning the possibility of the formation of an atom by successive addition of the individual electrons compel us to claim, first that the configurations of electrons are not only in mechanical equilibrium but also possess a certain stability in the sense required by ordinary mechanics, and secondly that the configurations employed must be of such a nature that transitions to these from other stationary states of the atom are possible. These requirements are not in general fulfilled by such simple configurations as electronic rings and they force us to look about for possibilities of more complicated motions. It will not be possible here to consider further these still open questions and I must content myself by referring to the discussion in my forthcoming paper. In closing, however, I should like to emphasize once more that in this lecture I have only intended to bring out certain general points of view lying at the basis of the spectral theory. In particular it was my intention to show that, in spite of the fundamental differences between these points of view and the ordinary conceptions of the phenomena of radiation, it still appears possible on the basis of the general correspondence between the spectrum and the motion in the atom to employ these conceptions in a certain sense as guides in the investigation of the spectra.

ESSAY III*

THE STRUCTURE OF THE ATOM AND THE PHYSICAL AND CHEMICAL PROPERTIES OF THE ELEMENTS

I. PRELIMINARY

In an address which I delivered to you about a year ago I described the main features of a theory of atomic structure which I shall attempt to develop this evening. In the meantime this theory has assumed more definite form, and in two recent letters to *Nature* I have given a somewhat further sketch of the development.† The results which I am about to present to you are of no final character; but I hope to be able to show you how this view renders a correlation of the various properties of the elements in such a way, that we avoid the difficulties which previously appeared to stand in the way of a simple and consistent explanation. Before proceeding, however, I must ask your forbearance if initially I deal with matters already known to you, but in order to introduce you to the subject it will first be necessary to give a brief description of the most important results which have been obtained in recent years in connection with the work on atomic structure.

---

*Address delivered before a joint meeting of the Physical and Chemical Societies in Copenhagen, October 18, 1921.

†*Nature*, March 24, and October 13, 1921.

The nuclear atom. The conception of atomic structure which will form the basis of all the following remarks is the so-called nuclear atom according to which an atom is assumed to consist of a nucleus surrounded by a number of electrons whose distances from one another and from the nucleus are very large compared to the dimensions of the particles themselves. The nucleus possesses almost the entire mass of the atom and has a positive charge of such a magnitude that the number of electrons in a neutral atom is equal to the number of the element in the periodic system, the so-called *atomic number*. This idea of the atom, which is due principally to Rutherford's fundamental researches on radioactive substances, exhibits extremely simple features, but just this simplicity appears at first sight to present difficulties in explaining the properties of the elements. When we treat this question on the basis of the ordinary mechanical and electrodynamical theories it is impossible to find a starting point for an explanation of the marked properties exhibited by the various elements, indeed not even of their permanency. On the one hand the particles of the atom apparently could not be at rest in a state of stable equilibrium, and on the other hand we should have to expect that every motion which might be present would give rise to the emission of electromagnetic radiation which would not cease until all the energy of the system had been emitted and all the electrons had fallen into the nucleus. A method of escaping from these difficulties has now been found in the application of ideas belonging to the quantum theory, the basis of which was laid by Planck in his celebrated work on the law of temperature radiation. This represented a radical departure from previous conceptions since it was the first instance in which the assumption of a discontinuity was employed in the formulation of the general laws of nature.

The postulates of the quantum theory. The quantum theory in the form in which it has been applied to the problems of atomic structure rests upon two postulates which have a direct bearing on the difficulties mentioned above. According to the first postulate there are certain states in which the atom can exist without emitting radiation, although the particles are supposed to have an accelerated motion relative to one another. These *stationary states* are, in addition, supposed to possess a peculiar kind of stability, so that it is impossible either to add energy to or remove energy from the atom except by a process involving a transition of the atom into another of these states. According to the second postulate each emission of radiation from the atom resulting from such a transition always consists of a train of purely harmonic waves. The frequency of these waves does not depend directly upon the motion of the atom, but is determined by a *frequency relation*, according to which the frequency multiplied by the universal constant introduced by Planck is equal to the total energy emitted during the process. For a transition between two stationary states for which the values of the energy of the atom before and after the emission of radiation are E' and E'' respectively, we have therefore

$$h\nu = E' - E'', \tag{1}$$

where h is Planck's constant and ν is the frequency of the emitted radiation. Time does not permit me to give a systematic survey of the quantum theory, the recent development of which has gone hand in hand with its applications to atomic structure. I shall therefore immediately proceed to the consideration of those applications of the theory which are of direct importance in connection with our subject.

Hydrogen atom. We shall commence by considering the simplest atom conceivable, namely, an atom consisting of a nucleus and one electron. If the charge on the nucleus corresponds to that of a single electron and the system consequently is neutral we have a hydrogen atom. Those developments of the quantum theory which have made possible its application to atomic structure started with the interpretation of the well-known simple spectrum emitted by hydrogen. This spectrum consists of a series of lines, the frequencies of which are given by the extremely simple Balmer formula

$$\nu = K\left(\frac{1}{(n'')^2} - \frac{1}{(n')^2}\right), \tag{2}$$

where n'' and n' are integers. According to the quantum theory we shall now assume that the atom possesses a series of stationary states characterized by a series of integers, and it can be seen how the frequencies given by formula (2) may be derived from the frequency relation if it is assumed that a hydrogen line is connected with a radiation emitted during a transition between two of these states corresponding to the numbers n' and n'', and if the energy in the nth state apart from an arbitrary additive constant is supposed to be given by the formula

$$E_n = -\frac{Kh}{n^2}. \tag{3}$$

The negative sign is used because the energy of the atom is measured most simply by the work required to remove the electron to infinite distance from the nucleus, and we shall assume that the numerical value of the expression on the right-hand side of formula (3) is just equal to this work.

As regards the closer description of the stationary states we find that the electron will very nearly describe an ellipse with the nucleus in the focus. The major axis of this ellipse is connected with the energy of the atom in a simple way, and corresponding to the energy values of the stationary states given by formula (3) there are a series of values for the major axis $2a$ of the orbit of the electron given by the formula

$$2a_n = \frac{n^2e^2}{hK}, \tag{4}$$

where e is the numerical value of the charge of the electron and the nucleus.

On the whole we may say that the spectrum of hydrogen shows us the *formation of the hydrogen atom*, since the stationary states may be regarded as different stages of a process by which the electron under the emission of radiation is bound in orbits of smaller and smaller dimensions corresponding to states with decreasing values of n. It will be seen that this view has certain characteristic features in common with the binding process of an electron to the nucleus if this were to take place according to the ordinary electrodynamics, but that our view differs from it in just such a way that it is possible to account for the observed properties of hydrogen. In particular it is seen that the final result of the binding process leads to a quite definite stationary state of the atom, namely that state for which $n = 1$. This state which corresponds to the minimum energy of the atom will be called the *normal state* of the atom. It may be stated here that the values of the energy of the atom and the major axis of the orbit of the electron which are found if we put $n = 1$ in formulae (3) and (4) are of the same order of magnitude as the values of the firmness of binding of electrons and of the dimensions of the atoms which have been obtained from experiments on the electrical and mechanical properties of gases. A more accurate check of formulae (3) and (4) can however not be obtained from such a comparison, because in such experiments hydrogen is not present in the form of simple atoms but as molecules.

The formal basis of the quantum theory consists not only of the frequency relation, but also of conditions which permit the determination of the stationary states of atomic systems. The latter conditions, like that assumed for the frequency, may be regarded as natural generalizations of that assumption regarding the interaction between simple electrodynamic systems and a surrounding field of electromagnetic radiation which forms the basis of Planck's theory of temperature radiation. I shall not here go further into the nature of these conditions but only mention that by their means the stationary states are characterized by a number of integers, the so-called *quantum numbers*. For a purely periodic motion like that assumed in the case of the hydrogen atom only a single quantum number is necessary for the determination of the stationary states. This number determines the energy of the atom and also the major axis of the orbit of the electron, but not its eccentricity. The energy in the various stationary states, if the small influence of the motion of the nucleus is neglected, is given by the following formula:

$$E_n = -\frac{2\pi^2 N^2 e^4 m}{n^2 h^2}, \tag{5}$$

where e and m are respectively the charge and the mass of the electron, and where for the sake of subsequent applications the charge on the nucleus has been designated by Ne.

For the atom of hydrogen $N = 1$, and a comparison with equation (3) leads to the following theoretical expression for K in formula (2), namely

$$K = \frac{2\pi^2 e^4 m}{h^3}. \tag{6}$$

This agrees with the empirical value of the constant for the spectrum of hydrogen within the limit of accuracy with which the various quantities can be determined.

Hydrogen spectrum and X-ray spectra. If in the above formula we put $N = 2$ which corresponds to an atom consisting of an electron revolving around a nucleus with a double charge, we get values for the energies in the stationary states, which are four times larger than the energies in the corresponding states of the hydrogen atom, and we obtain the following formula for the spectrum which would be emitted by such an atom:

$$\nu = 4K\left(\frac{1}{(n'')^2} - \frac{1}{(n')^2}\right). \tag{7}$$

This formula represents certain lines which have been known for some time and which had been attributed to hydrogen on account of the great similarity between formulae (2) and (7) since it had never been anticipated that two different substances could exhibit properties so closely resembling each other. According to the theory we may, however, expect that the emission of the spectrum given by (7) corresponds to the *first stage of the formation of the helium atom*, i.e. to the binding of a first electron by the doubly charged nucleus of this atom. This interpretation has been found to agree with more recent information. For instance it has been possible to obtain this spectrum from pure helium. I have dwelt on this point in order to show how this intimate connection between the properties of two elements, which at first sight might appear quite surprising, is to be regarded as an immediate expression of the characteristic simple structure of the nuclear atom. A short time after the elucidation of this question, new evidence of extraordinary interest was obtained of such a similarity between the properties of the elements. I refer to Moseley's fundamental researches on the X-ray spectra of the elements. Moseley found that these spectra varied in an extremely simple manner from one element to the next in the periodic system. It is well known that the lines of the X-ray spectra may be divided into groups corresponding to the different characteristic absorption regions for X-rays discovered by Barkla. As regards the K group which contains the most penetrating X-rays, Moseley found that the strongest line for all elements investigated could be represented by a formula which with a small simplification can be written

$$\nu = N^2 K \left(\frac{1}{1^2} - \frac{1}{2^2} \right). \tag{8}$$

K is the same constant as in the hydrogen spectrum, and N the atomic number. The great significance of this discovery lies in the fact that it would seem firmly to establish the view that this atomic number is equal to the number of electrons in the atom. This assumption had already been used as a basis for work on atomic structure and was first stated by van den Broek. While the significance of this aspect of Moseley's discovery was at once clear to all, it has on the other hand been more difficult to understand the very great similarity between the spectrum of hydrogen and the X-ray spectra. This similarity is shown, not only by the lines of the K group, but also by groups of less penetrating X-rays. Thus Moseley found for all the elements he investigated that the frequencies of the strongest line in the L group may be represented by a formula which with a simplification similar to that employed in formula (8) can be written

$$\nu = N^2 K \left(\frac{1}{2^2} - \frac{1}{3^2} \right). \tag{9}$$

Here again we obtain an expression for the frequency which corresponds to a line in the spectrum which would be emitted by the *binding of an electron to a nucleus, whose charge is* Ne.

The fine structure of the hydrogen lines. This similarity between the structure of the X-ray spectra and the hydrogen spectrum was still further extended in a very interesting manner by Sommerfeld's important theory of the fine structure of the hydrogen lines. The calculation given above of the energy in the stationary states of the hydrogen system, where each state is characterized by a single quantum number, rests upon the assumption that the orbit of the electron in the atom is simply periodic. This is, however, only approximately true. It is found that if the change in the mass of the electron due to its velocity is taken into consideration the orbit of the electron no longer remains a simple ellipse, but its motion may be described as a *central motion* obtained by superposing a slow and uniform rotation upon a simple periodic motion in a very nearly elliptical orbit. For a central motion of this kind the stationary states are characterized by *two quantum numbers*. In the case under consideration one of these may be so chosen that to a very close approximation it will determine the energy of the atom in the same manner as the quantum number previously used determined the energy in the case of a simple elliptical orbit. This quantum number which will always be denoted by n will therefore be called the "principal quantum number." Besides this condition, which to a very close approximation determines the major axis in the rotating and almost elliptical orbit, a second condition will be imposed upon the stationary states of a central orbit, namely that the angular momentum of the electron about the centre shall be equal to a whole multiple of Planck's constant divided by 2π. The whole number, which occurs as a factor in this expression, may be regarded as the second quantum number and will be denoted by k. The latter condition fixes the eccentricity of the rotating orbit which in the case of a simple periodic orbit was undetermined. It should be mentioned that the possible importance of the angular momentum in the quantum theory was pointed out by Nicholson before the application of this theory to the spectrum of hydrogen, and that a determination of the stationary states for the hydrogen atom similar to that employed by Sommerfeld was proposed almost simultaneously by Wilson, although the latter did not succeed in giving a physical application to his results.

The simplest description of the form of the rotating nearly elliptical electronic orbit in the hydrogen atom is obtained by considering the chord which passes through the focus and is perpendicular to the major axis, the so-called "parameter." The length $2p$ of this parameter is given to a very close approximation by an expression of exactly the same form as the expression for the major axis, except that k takes the place of n. Using the same notation as before we have therefore

$$2a = n^2 \frac{h^2}{2\pi^2 N e^2 m}, \quad 2p = k^2 \frac{h^2}{2\pi^2 N e^2 m}. \tag{10}$$

For each of the stationary states which had previously been denoted by a given value of n, we obtain therefore a set of stationary states corresponding to values of k from 1 to n. Instead of the simple formula (5) Sommerfeld found a more complicated expression for the energy in the stationary states which depends on k as well as n. Taking the variation of the mass of the electron with velocity into account and neglecting terms of higher order of magnitude he obtained

$$E_{n,k} = -\frac{2\pi^2 N^2 e^4 m}{n^2 h^2}\left[1 + \frac{4\pi^2 N^2 e^4}{h^2 c^2}\left(-\frac{3}{4n^2} + \frac{1}{nk}\right)\right], \tag{11}$$

where c is the velocity of light.

Corresponding to each of the energy values for the stationary states of the hydrogen atom given by the simple formula (5) we obtain n values differing only very little from one another, since the second term within the bracket is very small. With the aid of the general frequency relation (1) we therefore obtain a number of components with nearly coincident frequencies instead of each hydrogen line given by the simple formula (2). Sommerfeld has now shown that this calculation actually agrees with measurements of the fine structure. This agreement applies not only to the fine structure of the hydrogen lines which is very difficult to measure on account of the extreme proximity of the components, but it is also possible to account in detail for the fine structure of the helium lines given by formula (7) which has been very carefully investigated by Paschen. Sommerfeld in connection with this theory also pointed out that formula (11) could be applied to the X-ray spectra. Thus he showed that in the K and L groups pairs of lines appeared the differences of whose frequencies could be determined by the expression (11) for the energy in the stationary states which correspond to the binding of a single electron by a nucleus of charge Ne.

Periodic table. In spite of the great formal similarity between the X-ray spectra and the hydrogen spectrum indicated by these results a far-reaching difference must be assumed to exist between the processes which give rise to the appearance of these two types of spectra. While the emission of the hydrogen spectrum, like the emission of the ordinary optical spectra of other elements, may be assumed to be connected with the binding of an electron by an atom, observations on the appearance and absorption of X-ray spectra clearly indicate that these spectra are connected with a process which may be described as a *reorganization of the electronic arrangement* after a disturbance within the atom due to the effect of external agencies. We should therefore expect that the appearance of the X-ray spectra would depend not only upon the direct interaction between a single electron and the nucleus, but also on the manner in which the electrons are arranged in the completely formed atom.

The peculiar manner in which the properties of the elements vary with the atomic number, as expressed in the periodic system, provides a guide of great value in considering this latter problem. A simple survey of this system is given in fig. 1. The number preceding each element indicates the atomic number, and the elements within the various vertical columns form the different "periods" of the system. The lines, which connect pairs of elements in successive columns, indicate homologous properties of such elements. Compared with usual representations of the periodic system, this method, proposed more than twenty years ago by Julius Thomsen, of indicating the periodic variations in the properties of the elements is more suited for comparison with theories of atomic constitution. The meaning of the frames round certain sequences of elements within the later periods of the table will be explained later. They refer to certain characteristic features of the theory of atomic constitution.

In an explanation of the periodic system it is natural to assume a division of the electrons in the atom into dis-

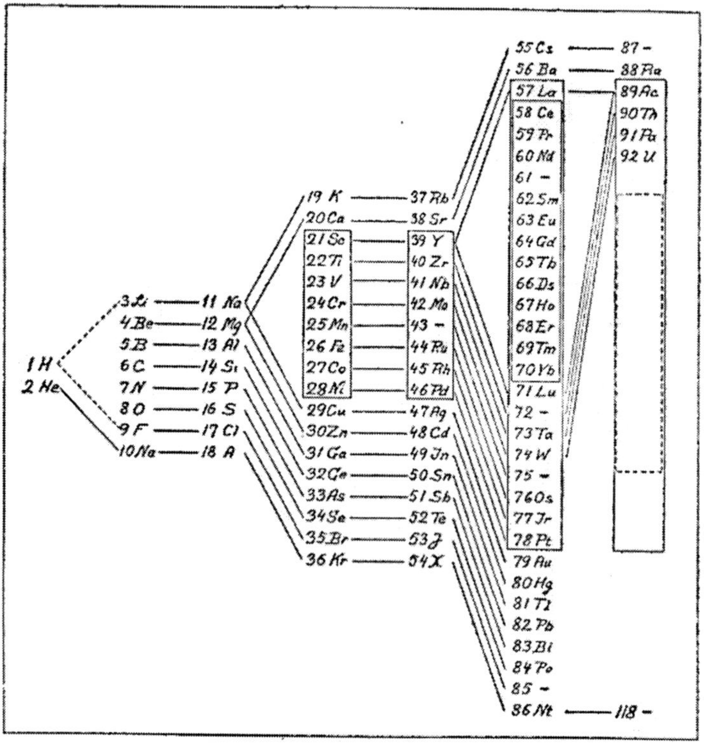

Fig. 1.

tinct groups in such a manner that the grouping of the elements in the system is attributed to the gradual formation of the groups of electrons in the atoms as the atomic number increases. Such a grouping of the electrons in the atom has formed a prominent part of all more detailed views of atomic structure ever since J. J. Thomson's famous attempt to explain the periodic system on the basis of an investigation of the stability of various electronic configurations. Although Thomson's assumption regarding the distribution of the positive electricity in the atom is not consistent with more recent experimental evidence, nevertheless his work has exerted great influence upon the later development of the atomic theory on account of the many original ideas which it contained.

With the aid of the information concerning the binding of electrons by the nucleus obtained from the theory of the hydrogen spectrum I attempted in the same paper in which this theory was set forth to sketch in broad outlines a picture of the structure of the nucleus atom. In this it was assumed that each electron in its normal state moved in a manner analogous to the motion in the last stages of the binding of a single electron by a nucleus. As in Thomson's theory, it was assumed that the electrons moved in circular orbits and that the electrons in each separate group during this motion occupied positions with reference to one another corresponding to the vertices of plane regular polygons. Such an arrangement is frequently described as a distribution of the electrons in "rings." By means of these assumptions it was possible to account for the orders of magnitude of the dimensions of the atoms as well as the firmness with which the electrons were bound by the atom, a measure of which may be obtained by means of experiments on the excitation of the various types of spectra. It was not possible, however, in this way to arrive at a detailed explanation of the characteristic properties of the elements even after it had become apparent from the results of Moseley and the work of Sommerfeld and others that this simple picture ought to be extended to include orbits in the fully formed atom characterized by higher quantum numbers corresponding to previous stages in the formation of the hydrogen atom. This point has been especially emphasized by Vegard.

The difficulty of arriving at a satisfactory picture of the atom is intimately connected with the difficulty of accounting for the pronounced "stability" which the properties of the elements demand. As I emphasized when considering the formation of the hydrogen atom, the postulates of the quantum theory aim directly at this point, but the results obtained in this way for an atom containing a single electron do not permit of a direct elucidation of problems like that of the distribution in groups of the electrons in an atom containing several electrons. If we imagine that the electrons in the groups of the atom are orientated relatively to one another at any moment, like the vertices of regular polygons, and rotating in either circles or ellipses, the postulates do not give sufficient information to determine the difference in the stability of electronic configurations with different numbers of electrons in the groups.

The peculiar character of stability of the atomic structure, demanded by the properties of the elements, is brought out in an interesting way by Kossel in two important papers.

In the first paper he shows that a more detailed explanation of the origin of the high frequency spectra can be obtained on the basis of the group structure of the atom. He assumes that a line in the X-ray spectrum is due to a process which may be described as follows: an electron is removed from the atom by some external action after which an electron in one of the other groups takes its place; this exchange of place may occur in as many ways as there are groups of more loosely bound electrons. This view of the origin of the characteristic X-rays afforded a simple explanation of the peculiar absorption phenomena observed. It has also led to the prediction of certain simple relations between the frequencies of the X-ray lines from one and the same element and has proved to be a suitable basis for the classification of the complete spectrum. However it has not been possible to develop a theory which reconciles in a satisfactory way Sommerfeld's work on the fine structure of the X-ray lines with Kossel's general scheme. As we shall see later the adoption of a new point of view when considering the stability of the atom renders it possible to bring the different results in a natural way in connection with one another.

In his second paper Kossel investigates the possibilities for an explanation of the periodic system on the basis of the atomic theory. Without entering further into the problem of the causes of the division of the electrons into groups, or the reasons for the different stability of the various electronic configurations, he points out in connection with ideas which had already played a part in Thomson's theory, how the periodic system affords evidence of a periodic appearance of especially stable configurations of electrons. These configurations appear in the neutral atoms of elements occupying the final position in each period in fig. 1, and the stability in question is assumed in order to explain not only the inactive chemical properties of these elements but also the characteristic active properties of the immediately preceding or succeeding elements. If we consider for instance an inactive gas like argon, the atomic number of which is 18, we must assume that the 18 electrons in the atom are arranged in an exceedingly regular configuration possessing a very marked stability. The pronounced electronegative character of the preceding element, chlorine, may then be explained by supposing the neutral atom which contains only 17 electrons to possess a tendency to capture an additional electron. This gives rise to a negative chlorine ion with a configuration of 18 electrons similar to that occurring in the neutral argon atom. On the other hand the marked electropositive character of potassium may be explained by supposing one of the 19 electrons in the neutral atom to be as it were superfluous, and that this electron therefore is easily lost; the rest of the atom forming a positive ion of potassium having a constitution similar to that of the argon atom. In a corresponding manner it is possible to account for the electronegative and electropositive character of elements like sulphur and calcium, whose atomic numbers are 16 and 20. In contrast to chlorine and potassium these elements are divalent, and the stable configuration of 18 electrons is formed by the addition of two electrons to the sulphur atom and by the loss of two electrons from the calcium atom. Developing these ideas Kossel has succeeded not only in giving interesting explanations of a large number of chemical facts, but has also been led to certain general conclusions about the grouping of the electrons in elements belonging to the first periods of the periodic system, which in certain respects are in conformity with the results to be discussed in the following paragraphs. Kossel's work was later continued in an interesting manner by Ladenburg with special reference to the grouping of the electrons in atoms of elements belonging to the later periods of the periodic table. It will be seen that Ladenburg's conclusions also exhibit points of similarity with the results which we shall discuss later.

Recent atomic models. Up to the present time it has not been possible to obtain a satisfactory account based upon a consistent application of the quantum theory to the nuclear atom of the ultimate cause of the pronounced stability of certain arrangements of electrons. Nevertheless it has been apparent for some time that the solution should be sought for by investigating the possibilities of a *spatial distribution of the electronic orbits* in the atom instead of limiting the investigation to configurations in which all electrons belonging to a particular group move in the same plane as was assumed for simplicity in my first papers on the structure of the atom. The necessity of assuming a spatial distribution of the configurations of electrons has been drawn attention to by various writers. Born and Landé, in connection with their investigations of the structure and properties of crystals, have pointed out that the assumption of spatial configurations appears necessary for an explanation of these properties. Landé has pursued this question still further, and as will be mentioned later has proposed a number of different "spatial atomic models" in which the electrons in each separate group of the atom at each moment form configurations possessing regular polyhedral symmetry. These models constitute in certain respects a distinct advance, although they have not led to decisive results on questions of the stability of atomic structure.

The importance of spatial electronic configurations has, in addition, been pointed out by Lewis and Langmuir in connection with their atomic models. Thus Lewis, who in several respects independently came to the same conclusions as Kossel, suggested that the number 8 characterizing the first groups of the periodic system might indicate a constitution of the outer atomic groups where the electrons within each group formed a configuration like the corners of a cube. He emphasized how a configuration of this kind leads to instructive models of the molecular structure of chemical combinations. It is to be remarked, however, that such a "static" model of electronic configuration will not be possible if we assume the forces within the atom to be due exclusively to the electric charges of the particles. Langmuir, who has attempted to develop Lewis' conceptions still further and to account not only for the occurrence of the first octaves, but also for the longer periods of the periodic system, supposes therefore the structure of the atoms to be governed by forces whose nature is unknown to us. He conceives the atom to possess a "cellular structure," so that each electron is in advance assigned a place in a cell and these cells are arranged in shells in such a manner, that the various shells from the nucleus of the atom outward contain exactly the same number of places as the periods in the periodic system proceeding in the direction of increasing atomic number. Langmuir's work has attracted much attention among chemists, since it has to some extent thrown light on the conceptions with which empirical chemical science is concerned. On his theory the explanation of the properties of the various elements is based on a number of postulates about the structure of the atoms formulated for that purpose. Such a descriptive theory is sharply differentiated from one where an attempt is made to explain the specific properties of the elements with the aid of general laws applying to the interaction between the particles in each atom. The principal task of this lecture will consist in an attempt to show that an advance along these lines appears by no means hopeless, but on the contrary that with the aid of a consistent application of the postulates of the quantum theory it actually appears possible to obtain an insight into the structure and stability of the atom.

II. SERIES SPECTRA AND THE CAPTURE OF ELECTRONS BY ATOMS

We attack the problem of atomic constitution by asking the question: "How may an atom be formed by the successive capture and binding of the electrons one by one in the field of force surrounding the nucleus?"

Before attempting to answer this question it will first be necessary to consider in more detail what the quantum theory teaches us about the general character of the binding process. We have already seen how the hydrogen spectrum gives us definite information about the course of this process of binding the electron by the nucleus. In considering the formation of the atoms of other elements we have also in their spectra sources for the elucidation of the formation processes, but the direct information obtained in this way is not so complete as in the case of the hydrogen atom. For an element of atomic number N the process of formation may be regarded as occurring in N stages, corresponding with the successive binding of N electrons in the field of the nucleus. A spectrum must be assumed to correspond to each of these binding processes; but only for the first two elements, hydrogen and helium, do we possess a detailed knowledge of these spectra. For other elements of higher atomic number, where several spectra will be connected with the formation of the atom, we are at present acquainted with only two types, called the "arc" and "spark" spectra respectively, according to the experimental conditions of excitation. Although these spectra show a much more complicated structure than the hydrogen spectrum, given by formula (2) and the helium spectrum given by formula (7), nevertheless in many cases it has been possible to find simple laws for the frequencies exhibiting a close analogy with the laws expressed by these formulae.

Arc and spark spectra. If for the sake of simplicity we disregard the complex structure shown by the lines of most spectra (occurrence of doublets, triplets etc.), the frequency of the lines of many arc spectra can be represented to a close approximation by the Rydberg formula

$$\nu = \frac{K}{(n'' + \alpha_{k''})^2} - \frac{K}{(n' + \alpha_{k'})^2}, \tag{12}$$

where n' and n'' are integral numbers, K the same constant as in the hydrogen spectrum, while $\alpha_{k'}$ and $\alpha_{k''}$ are two constants belonging to a set characteristic of the element. A spectrum with a structure of this kind is, like the hydrogen spectrum, called a series spectrum, since the lines can be arranged into series in which the frequencies converge to definite limiting values. These series are for example represented by formula (12) if, using two definite constants for $\alpha_{k''}$ and $\alpha_{k'}$, n'' remains unaltered, while n' assumes a series of successive, gradually increasing integral values.

Formula (12) applies only approximately, but it is always found that the frequencies of the spectral lines can be written, as in formulae (2) and (12), as a difference of two functions of integral numbers. Thus the latter formula applies accurately, if the quantities α_k are not considered as constants, but as representatives of a set of series of numbers $\alpha_k(n)$ characteristic of the element, whose values for increasing n within each series quickly approach a constant limiting value. The fact that the frequencies of the spectra always appear as the difference of two terms, the so-called "spectral terms," from the combinations of which the complete spectrum is formed, has been pointed out by Ritz, who with the establishment of the combination principle has greatly advanced the study of the spectra. The quantum theory offers an immediate interpretation of this principle, since, according to the frequency relation we are led to consider the lines as due to transitions between stationary states of the atom, just as in the hydrogen spectrum, only in the spectra of the other elements we have to do not with a single series of stationary states, but with a set of such series. From formula (12) we thus obtain for an arc spectrum—if we temporarily disregard the structure of the individual lines—information about an ensemble of stationary states, for which the energy of the atom in the nth state of the kth series is given by

$$E_k(n) = -\frac{Kh}{(n+\alpha_k)^2} \tag{13}$$

very similar to the simple formula (3) for the energy in the stationary states of the hydrogen atom.

As regards the spark spectra, the structure of which has

been cleared up mainly by Fowler's investigations, it has been possible in the case of many elements to express the frequencies approximately by means of a formula of exactly the same type as (12), only with the difference that K, just as in the helium spectrum given by formula (7), is replaced by a constant, which is four times as large. For the spark spectra, therefore, the energy values in the corresponding stationary states of the atom will be given by an expression of the same type as (13), only with the difference that K is replaced by $4K$.

This remarkable similarity between the structure of these types of spectra and the simple spectra given by (2) and (7) is explained simply by assuming the arc spectra to be connected with the *last stage in the formation of the neutral atom* consisting in the capture and binding of the Nth electron. On the other hand the spark spectra are connected with the *last stage but one in the formation of the atom*, namely the binding of the $(N-1)$th electron. In these cases the field of force in which the electron moves will be much the same as that surrounding the nucleus of a hydrogen or helium atom respectively, at least in the earlier stages of the binding process, where during the greater part of its revolution it moves at a distance from the nucleus which is large in proportion to the dimensions of the orbits of the electrons previously bound. From analogy with formula (3) giving the stationary states of the hydrogen atom, we shall therefore assume that the numerical value of the expression on the right-hand side of (13) will be equal to the work required to remove the last captured electron from the atom, the binding of which gives rise to the arc spectrum of the element.

Series diagram. While the origin of the arc and spark spectra was to this extent immediately interpreted on the basis of the original simple theory of the hydrogen spectrum, it was Sommerfeld's theory of the fine structure of the hydrogen lines which first gave us a clear insight into the characteristic difference between the hydrogen spectrum and the spark spectrum of helium on the one hand, and the arc and spark spectra of other elements on the other. When we consider the binding not of the first but of the subsequent electrons in the atom, the orbit of the electron under consideration—at any rate in the latter stages of the binding process where the electron last bound comes into intimate interaction with those previously bound—will no longer be to a near approximation a closed ellipse, but on the contrary will to a first approximation be a central orbit of the same type as in the hydrogen atom, when we take into account the change with velocity in the mass of the electron. This motion, as we have seen, may be resolved into a plane periodic motion upon which a uniform rotation is superposed in the plane of the orbit; only the superposed rotation will in this case be comparatively much more rapid and the deviation of the periodic orbit from an ellipse much greater than in the case of the hydrogen atom. For an orbit of this type the stationary states, just as in the theory of the fine structure, will be determined by two quantum numbers which we shall denote by n and k, connected in a very simple manner with the kinematic properties of the orbit. For brevity I shall only mention that while the quantum number k is connected with the value of the constant angular momentum of the electron about the centre in the simple manner previously indicated, the determination of the principal quantum number n requires an investigation of the whole course of the orbit and for an arbitrary central orbit will not be related in a simple way to the dimensions of the rotating periodic orbit if this deviates essentially from a Keplerian ellipse.

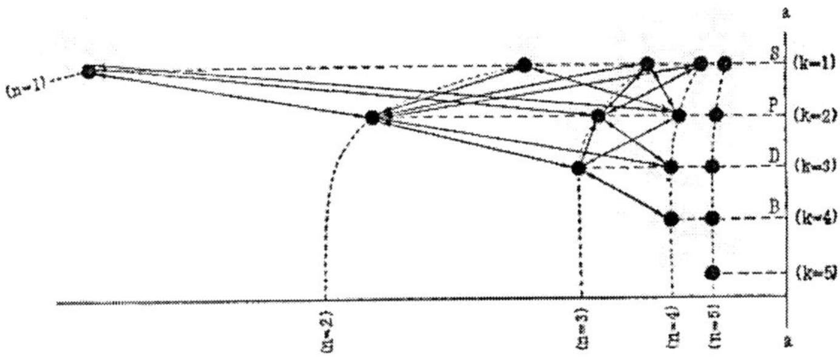

Fig. 2.

These results are represented in fig. 2 which is a reproduction of an illustration I have used on a previous occasion (see Essay II, page 46), and which gives a survey of the origin of the sodium spectrum. The black dots represent the stationary states corresponding to the various series of spectral terms, shown on the right by the letters S, P, D and B.

These letters correspond to the usual notations employed in spectroscopic literature and indicate the nature of the series (sharp series, principal series, diffuse series, etc.) obtained by combinations of the corresponding spectral terms. The distances of the separate points from the vertical line at the right of the figure are proportional to the numerical value of the energy of the atom given by equation (13). The oblique, black arrows indicate finally the transitions between the stationary states giving rise to the appearance of the lines in the commonly observed sodium spectrum. The values of n and k attached to the various states indicate the quantum numbers, which, according to Sommerfeld's theory, from a preliminary consideration might be regarded as characterizing the orbit of the outer electron. For the sake of convenience the states which were regarded as corresponding to the same value of n are connected by means of dotted lines, and these are so drawn that their vertical asymptotes correspond to the terms in the hydrogen spectrum which belong to the same value of the principal quantum number. The course of the curves illustrates how the deviation from the hydrogen terms may be expected to decrease with increasing values of k, corresponding to states, where the minimum distance between the electron in its revolution and the nucleus constantly increases.

It should be noted that even though the theory represents the principal features of the structure of the series spectra it has not yet been possible to give a detailed account of the spectrum of any element by a closer investigation of the electronic orbits which may occur in a simple field of force possessing central symmetry. As I have mentioned already the lines of most spectra show a complex structure. In the sodium spectrum for instance the lines of the principal series are doublets indicating that to each P-term not one stationary state, but two such states correspond with slightly different values of the energy. This difference is so little that it would not be recognizable in a diagram on the same scale as fig. 2. The appearance of these doublets is undoubtedly due to the small deviations from central symmetry of the field of force originating from the inner system in consequence of which the general type of motion of the external electron will possess a more complicated character than that of a simple central motion. As a result the stationary states must be characterized by more than two quantum numbers, in the same way that the occurrence of deviations of the orbit of the electron in the hydrogen atom from a simple periodic orbit requires that the stationary states of this atom shall be characterized by more than one quantum number. Now the rules of the quantum theory lead to the introduction of a third quantum number through the condition that the resultant angular momentum of the atom, multiplied by 2π, is equal to an entire multiple of Planck's constant. This determines the orientation of the orbit of the outer electron relative to the axis of the inner system.

In this way Sommerfeld, Landé and others have shown that it is possible not only to account in a formal way for the complex structure of the lines of the series spectra, but also to obtain a promising interpretation of the complicated effect of external magnetic fields on this structure. We shall not enter here on these problems but shall confine ourselves to the problem of the fixation of the two quantum numbers n and k, which to a first approximation describe the orbit of the outer electron in the stationary states, and whose determination is a matter of prime importance in the following discussion of the formation of the atom. In the determination of these numbers we at once encounter difficulties of a profound nature, which—as we shall see—are intimately connected with the question of the remarkable stability of atomic structure. I shall here only remark that the values of the quantum number n, given in the figure, undoubtedly cannot be retained, neither for the S nor the P series. On the other hand, so far as the values employed for the quantum number k are concerned, it may be stated with certainty, that the interpretation of the properties of the orbits, which they indicate, is correct. A starting point for the investigation of this question has been obtained from considerations of an entirely different kind from those previously mentioned, which have made it possible to establish a close connection between the motion in the atom and the appearance of spectral lines.

Correspondence principle. So far as the principles of the quantum theory are concerned, the point which has been emphasized hitherto is the radical departure of these principles from our usual conceptions of mechanical and electrodynamical phenomena. As I have attempted to show in recent years, it appears possible, however, to adopt a point of view which suggests that the quantum theory may, nevertheless, be regarded as a rational generalization of our ordinary conceptions. As may be seen from the postulates of the quantum theory, and particularly the frequency relation, a direct connection between the spectra and the motion of the kind required by the classical dynamics is excluded, but at the same time the form of these postulates leads us to another relation of a remarkable nature. Let us consider an electrodynamic system and inquire into the nature of the radiation which would result from the motion of the system on the basis of the ordinary conceptions. We imagine the motion to be decomposed into purely harmonic oscillations, and the radiation is assumed to consist of the simultaneous emission of series of electromagnetic waves possessing the same frequency as these harmonic components and intensities which depend upon the amplitudes of the components. An investigation of the formal basis of the quantum theory shows us now, that it is possible to trace the question of the origin of the radiation processes which accompany the various transitions back to an investigation of the various harmonic components, which appear in the motion of the atom. The possibility, that a particular transition shall occur, may be regarded as being due to the presence of a definitely assignable "corresponding" component in the motion. This principle of correspondence at the same time throws light upon a question mentioned several times previously, namely the relation between the number of quantum numbers, which must be used to describe the stationary states of an atom, and the types to which the orbits of the electrons belong. The classification of these types can be based very simply on a decomposition of the motion into its harmonic components. Time does not permit me to consider this question any further, and I shall confine myself to a statement of some simple conclusions, which the correspondence principle permits us to draw concerning the occurrence of transitions between various pairs of stationary states. These conclusions are of decisive importance in the subsequent argument.

The simplest example of such a conclusion is obtained by considering an atomic system, which contains a particle describing a *purely periodic orbit*, and where the stationary states are characterized by a single quantum number n. In this case the motion can according to Fourier's theorem be decomposed into a simple series of harmonic oscillations whose frequency may be written $\tau\omega$, where τ is a whole number, and ω is the frequency of revolution in the orbit. It can now be shown that a transition between two stationary states, for which the values of the quantum number are respectively equal to n' and n'', will correspond to a harmonic component, for which $\tau = n' - n''$. This throws at once light upon the remarkable difference which exists between the possibilities of transitions between the stationary states of a hydrogen atom on the one hand and of a simple system consisting of an electric particle capable of executing simple harmonic oscillations about a position of equilibrium on the other. For the latter system, which is frequently called a Planck oscillator, the energy in the stationary states is determined by the familiar formula $E = nh\omega$, and with the aid of the frequency relation we obtain therefore for the radiation which will be emitted during a transition between two stationary states $\nu = (n' - n'')\omega$. Now, an important assumption, which is not only essential in Planck's theory of temperature radiation, but which also appears necessary to account for the molecular absorption in the infra-red region of radiation, states that a harmonic oscillator will only emit and absorb radiation, for which the frequency ν is equal to the frequency of oscillation ω of the oscillator. We are therefore compelled to assume that in the case of the oscillator transitions can occur only between stationary states which are characterized by quantum numbers differing by only one unit, while in the hydrogen spectrum represented by formula (2) all possible transitions could take place between the stationary states given by formula (5). From the point of view of the principle of correspondence it is seen, however, that this apparent difficulty is explained by the occurrence in the motion of the hydrogen atom, as opposed to the motion of the oscillator, of harmonic components corresponding to values of τ, which are different from 1; or using a terminology well known from acoustics, there appear overtones in the motion of the hydrogen atom.

Another simple example of the application of the correspondence principle is afforded by a *central motion*, to the investigation of which the explanation of the series spectra in the first approximation may be reduced. Referring once more to the figure of the sodium spectrum, we see that the black arrows, which correspond to the spectral lines appearing under the usual conditions of excitation, only connect pairs of points in consecutive rows. Now it is found that this remarkable limitation of the occurrence of combinations between spectral terms may quite naturally be explained by an investigation of the harmonic components into which a central motion can be resolved. It can readily be shown that such a motion can be decomposed into two series of harmonic components, whose frequencies can be expressed by $\tau\omega + \sigma$ and $\tau\omega - \sigma$ respectively, where τ is a whole number, ω the frequency of revolution in the rotating periodic orbit and σ the frequency of the superposed rotation. These components correspond with transitions where the principal number n decreases by τ units, while the quantum number k decreases or increases, respectively, by one unit, corresponding exactly with the transitions indicated by the black arrows in the figure. This may be considered as a very important result, because we may say, that the quantum theory, which for the first time has offered a simple interpretation of the fundamental principle of combination of spectral lines has at the same time removed the mystery which has hitherto adhered to the application of this principle on account of the apparent capriciousness of the appearance of predicted combination lines. Especially attention may be drawn to the simple interpretation which the quantum theory offers of the appearance observed by Stark and his collaborators of certain new series of lines, which do not appear under ordinary circumstances, but which are excited when the emitting atoms are subject to intense external electric fields. In fact, on the correspondence principle this is immediately explained from an examination of the perturbations in the motion of the outer electron which give rise to the appearance in this motion—besides the harmonic components already present in a simple central orbit—of a number of constituent harmonic vibrations of new type and of amplitudes proportional to the intensity of the external forces.

It may be of interest to note that an investigation of the limitation of the possibility of transitions between stationary states, based upon a simple consideration of conservation of angular momentum during the process of radiation, does not, contrary to what has previously been supposed (compare Essay II, page 94), suffice to throw light on the remarkably simple structure of series spectra illustrated by the figure. As mentioned above we must assume that the "complexity" of the spectral terms, corresponding to given values of n and k, which we witness in the fine structure of the spectral lines, may be ascribed to states, corresponding to different values of this angular momentum, in which the plane of the electronic orbit is orientated in a different manner, relative to the configuration of the previously bound electrons in the atom. Considerations of conservation of angular momentum can, in connection with the series spectra, therefore only contribute to an understanding of the limitation of the possibilities of combination observed in the peculiar laws applying to the number of components in the complex structure of the lines. So far as the last question is concerned, such considerations offer a direct support for the consequences of the correspondence principle.

III. FORMATION OF ATOMS AND THE PERIODIC TABLE

A correspondence has been shown to exist between the motion of the electron last captured and the occurrence of transitions between the stationary states corresponding to the various stages of the binding process. This fact gives a point of departure for a choice between the numerous possibilities which present themselves when considering the formation of the atoms by the successive capture and binding of the electrons. Among the processes which are conceivable and which according to the quantum theory might occur in the atom we shall reject those whose occurrence cannot be regarded as consistent with a correspondence of the required nature.

First Period. Hydrogen—Helium. It will not be necessary to concern ourselves long with the question of the constitution of the hydrogen atom. From what has been said previously we may assume that the final result of the process of *binding of the first electron* in any atom will be a stationary state, where the energy of the atom is given by (5), if we put $n = 1$, or more precisely by formula (11), if we put $n = 1$ and $k = 1$. The orbit of the electron will be a circle whose radius will be given by formulae (10), if n and k are each put equal to 1. Such an orbit will be called a 1-quantum orbit, and in general an orbit for which the principal quantum number has a given value n will be called an n-quantum orbit. Where it is necessary to differentiate between orbits corresponding to various values of the quantum number k, a central orbit, characterized by given values of the quantum numbers n and k, will be referred to as an n_k orbit.

In the question of the constitution of the helium atom we meet the much more complicated problem of the *binding of the second electron.* Information about this binding process may, however, be obtained from the arc spectrum of helium. This spectrum, as opposed to most other simple spectra, consists of two complete systems of lines with frequencies given by formulae of the type (12). On this account helium was at first assumed to be a mixture of two different gases, "orthohelium" and "parhelium," but now we know that the two spectra simply mean that the binding of the second electron can occur in two different ways. A theoretical explanation of the main features of the helium spectrum has recently been attempted in an interesting paper by Landé. He supposes the emission of the orthohelium spectrum to be due to transitions between stationary states where both electrons move in the same plane and revolve in the same sense. The parhelium spectrum, on the other hand, is ascribed by him to stationary states where the planes of the orbits form an angle with each other. Dr Kramers and I have made a closer investigation of the interaction between the two orbits in the different stationary states. The results of our investigation which was begun several years before the appearance of Landé's work have not yet been published. Without going into details I may say, that even though our results in several respects differ materially from those of Landé (compare Essay II, page 85), we agree with his general conclusions concerning the origin of the orthohelium and parhelium spectra.

The final result of the binding of the second electron is intimately related to the origin of the two helium spectra. Important information on this point has been obtained recently by Franck and his co-workers. As is well known he has thrown light upon many features of the structure of the atom and of the origin of spectra by observing the effect of bombarding atoms by electrons of various velocities. A short time ago these experiments showed that the impact of electrons could bring helium into a "metastable" state from which the atom cannot return to its normal state by means of a simple transition accompanied by the emission of radiation, but only by means of a process analogous to a chemical reaction involving interaction with atoms of other elements. This result is closely connected with the fact that the binding of the second electron can occur in two different ways, as is shown by the occurrence of two distinct spectra. Thus it is evident from Franck's experiments that the normal state of the atom is the last stage in the binding process involving the emission of the parhelium spectrum by which the electron last captured as well as the one first captured will be bound in a 1_1 orbit. The metastable state, on the contrary, is the final stage of the process giving the orthohelium spectrum. In this case the second electron, as opposed to the first, will move in a 2_1 orbit. This corresponds to a firmness of binding which is about six times less than for the electron in the normal state of the atom.

If we now consider somewhat more closely this apparently surprising result, it is found that a clear grasp of it may be obtained from the point of view of correspondence. It can be shown that the coherent class of motions to which the orthohelium orbits belong does not contain a 1_1 orbit. If on the whole we would claim the existence of a state where the two electrons move in 1_1 orbits in the same plane, and if in addition it is claimed that the motion should possess the periodic properties necessary for the definition of stationary states, then there seems that no possibility is afforded other than the assumption that the two electrons move around the nucleus in one and the same orbit, in such a manner that at each moment they are situated at the ends of a diameter. This extremely simple ring-configuration might be expected to correspond to the firmest possible binding of the electrons in the atom, and it was on this account proposed as a model for the helium atom in my first paper on atomic structure. If, however, we inquire about the possibility of a transition from one of the orthohelium states to a configuration of this type we meet conditions which are very different from those which apply to transitions between two of the orthohelium orbits. In fact, the occurrence of each of these transitions is due to the existence of well-defined corresponding constituent harmonic vibration in the central orbits which the outer electron describes in the class of motions to which the stationary states belong. The transition we have to discuss, on the other hand, is one by which the last captured electron is transferred from a state in which it is moving "outside" the other to a state in which it moves round the nucleus on equal terms with the other electron. Now it is impossible to find a series of simple intermediate forms for the motion of those two electrons in which the orbit of the last captured electron exhibits a sufficient similarity to a central motion that for this transition there could be a correspondence of the necessary kind. It is therefore evident, that where the two electrons move in the same plane, the electron captured last cannot be bound firmer than in a 2_1 orbit. If, on the other hand, we consider the binding process which accompanies the emission of the parhelium spectrum and where the electrons in the stationary states move in orbits whose planes form angles with one another we meet essentially different conditions. A corresponding intimate change in the interaction between the electron last captured and the one previously bound is not required here for the two electrons in the atom to become equivalent. We may therefore imagine the last stage of the binding process to take place in a manner similar to those stages corresponding to transitions between orbits characterized by greater values of n and k.

In the *normal state of the helium atom* the two electrons must be assumed to move in equivalent 1_1 orbits. As a first approximation these may be described as two circular orbits, whose planes make an angle of 120° with one another, in agreement with the conditions which the angular momentum of an atom according to the quantum theory must satisfy. On account of the interaction between the two electrons these planes at the same time turn slowly around the fixed impulse axis of the atom. Starting from a distinctly different point of view Kemble has recently suggested a similar model for the helium atom. He has at the same time directed attention to a possible type of motion of very marked symmetry in which the electrons during their entire revolution assume symmetrical positions with reference to a fixed axis. Kemble has not, however, investigated this motion further. Previous to the appearance of this paper Kramers had commenced a closer investigation of precisely this type of motion in order to find out to what extent it was possible from such a calculation to account for the firmness with which the electrons are bound in the helium atom, that is to account for the ionization potential. Early measurements of this potential had given values corresponding approximately to that which would result from the ring-configuration already mentioned. This requires 17/8 as much work to remove a single electron as is necessary to remove an electron from the hydrogen atom in its normal state. As the theoretical value for the latter amount of work—which for the sake of simplicity will be represented by W—corresponds to an ionization potential of 13.53 volts, the ionization potential of helium would be expected to be 28.8 volts. Recent and more accurate determinations, however, have given a value for the ionization potential of helium which is considerably lower and lies in the neighbourhood of 25 volts. This showed therefore the untenability of the ring-configuration quite independently of any other considerations. A careful investigation of the spatial atomic configuration requires elaborate calculation, and Kramers has not yet obtained final results. With the approximation to which they have been so far completed the calculations point to the possibility of an agreement with the experimental results. The final result may be awaited with great interest, since it offers in the simplest case imaginable a test of the principles by which we are attempting to determine stationary states of atoms containing more than one electron.

Hydrogen and helium, as seen in the survey of the periodic system given in fig. 1, together form the first period in the system of elements, since helium is the first of the inactive gases. The great difference in the chemical properties of hydrogen and helium is closely related to the great difference in the nature of the binding of the electron. This is directly indicated by the spectra and ionization potentials. While helium possesses the highest known ionization potential of all the elements, the binding of the electron in the hydrogen atom is sufficiently loose to account for the tendency of hydrogen to form positive ions in aqueous solutions and chemical combinations. Further consideration of this particular question requires, however, a comparison between the nature and firmness of the electronic configurations of other atoms, and it can therefore not be discussed at the moment.

Second Period. Lithium—Neon. When considering the atomic structure of elements which contain more than two electrons in the neutral atom, we shall assume first of all that what has previously been said about the formation of the helium atom will in the main features also apply to the capture and binding of the first two electrons. These electrons may, therefore, in the normal state of the atom be regarded as moving in equivalent orbits characterized by the quantum symbol 1_1. We obtain direct information about the *binding of the third electron* from the spectrum of lithium. This spectrum shows the existence of a number of series of stationary states, where the firmness with which the last captured electron is bound is very nearly the same as in the stationary states of the hydrogen atom. These states correspond to orbits where k is greater than or equal to 2, and where the last captured electron moves entirely outside the region where the first two electrons move. But in addition this spectrum gives us information about a series of states corresponding to $k = 1$ in which the energy differs essentially from the corresponding stationary states of the hydrogen atom. In these states the last captured electron, even if it remains at a considerable distance from the nucleus during the greater part of its revolution, will at certain moments during the revolution approach to a distance from the nucleus which is of the same order of magnitude as the dimensions of the orbits of the previously bound electrons. On this account the electrons will be bound with a firmness which is considerably greater than that with which the electrons are bound in the stationary states of the hydrogen atom corresponding to the same value of n.

Now as regards the lithium spectrum as well as the other alkali spectra we are so fortunate (see page 48) as to possess definite evidence about the normal state of the atom from experiments on selective absorption. In fact these experiments tell us that the first member of the sequence of S-terms corresponds to this state. This term corresponds to a strength of binding which is only a little more than a third of that of the hydrogen atom. We must therefore conclude that the outer electron in the normal state of the lithium atom moves in a 2_1 orbit, just as the outer electron in the metastable state of the helium atom. The reason why the binding of the outer electron cannot proceed to an orbit characterized by a smaller value for the total quantum number may also be considered as analogous in the two cases. In fact, a transition by which the third electron in the lithium atom was ultimately bound in a 1_1 orbit would lead to a state in the atom in which the electron would play an equivalent part with the two electrons previously bound. Such a process would be of a type entirely different from the transitions between the stationary states connected with the emission of the lithium spectrum, and would, contrary to these, not exhibit a correspondence with a harmonic component in the motion of the atom.

We obtain, therefore, a picture of the formation and structure of the lithium atom which offers a natural explanation of the great difference of the chemical properties of lithium from those of helium and hydrogen. This difference is at once explained by the fact that the firmness by which the last captured electron is bound in its 2_1 orbit in the lithium atom is only about a third of that with which the electron in the hydrogen atom is held, and almost five times smaller than the firmness of the binding of the electrons in the helium atom.

What has been said here applies not alone to the formation of the lithium atom, but may also be assumed to apply to the binding of the third electron in every atom, so that in contrast to the first two electrons which move in 1_1 orbits this may be assumed to move in a 2_1 orbit. As regards the *binding of the fourth, fifth and sixth electrons* in the atom, we do not possess a similar guide as no simple series spectra are known of beryllium, boron and carbon. Although conclusions of the same degree of certainty cannot be reached it seems possible, however, to arrive at results consistent with general physical and chemical evidence by proceeding by means of considerations of the same kind as those applied to the binding of the first three electrons. In fact, we shall assume that the fourth, fifth and sixth electrons will be bound in 2_1 orbits. The reason why the binding of a first electron in an orbit of this type will not prevent the capture of the others in two quanta orbits may be ascribed to the fact that 2_1 orbits are not circular but very eccentric; For example, the 3rd electron cannot keep the remaining electrons away from the inner system in the same way in which the first two electrons bound in the lithium atom prevent the third from being bound in a 1-quantum orbit. Thus we shall expect that the 4th, 5th and 6th electrons in a similar way to the 3rd will at certain moments of their revolution enter into the region where the first two bound electrons move. We must not imagine, however, that these visits into the inner system take place at the same time, but that the four electrons visit the nucleus separately at equal intervals of time. In earlier work on atomic structure it was supposed that the electrons in the various groups in the atom moved in separate regions within the atom and that at each moment the electrons within each separate group were arranged in configurations possessing symmetry like that of a regular polygon or polyhedron. Among other things this involved that the electrons in each group were supposed to be at the point of the orbit nearest the nucleus at the same time. A structure of this kind may be described as one where the motions of the electrons within the groups are coupled together in a manner which is largely independent of the interaction between the various groups. On the contrary, the characteristic feature of a structure like that I have suggested is the *intimate coupling between the motions of the electrons in the various groups* characterized by different quantum numbers, as well as the *greater independence in the mode of binding within one and the same group of electrons* the orbits of which are characterized by the same quantum number. In emphasizing this last feature I have two points in mind. Firstly the smaller effect of the presence of previously bound electrons on the firmness of binding of succeeding electrons in the same group. Secondly the way in which the motions of the electrons within the group reflect the independence both of the processes by which the group can be formed and by which it can be reorganized by change of position of the different electrons in the atom after a disturbance by external forces. The last point will be considered more closely when we deal with the origin and nature of the X-ray spectra; for the present we shall continue the consideration of the structure of the atom to which we are led by the investigation of the processes connected with the successive capture of the electrons.

The preceding considerations enable us to understand the fact that the two elements beryllium and boron immediately succeeding lithium can appear electropositively with 2 and 3 valencies respectively in combination with other substances. For like the third electron in the lithium atom, the last captured electrons in these elements will be much more lightly bound than the first two electrons. At the same time we understand why the electropositive character of these elements is less marked than in the case of lithium, since the electrons in the 2-quanta orbits will be much more firmly bound on account of the stronger field in which they are moving. New conditions arise, however, in the case of the next element, carbon, as this element in its typical chemical combinations cannot be supposed to occur as an ion, but rather as a neutral atom. This must be assumed to be due not only to the great firmness in the binding of the electrons but also to be an essential consequence of the symmetrical configuration of the electrons.

With the binding of the 4th, 5th and 6th electrons in 2_1 orbits, the spatial symmetry of the regular configuration of the orbits must be regarded as steadily increasing, until with the binding of the 6th electron the orbits of the four last bound electrons may be expected to form an exceptionally symmetrical configuration in which the normals to the planes of the orbits occupy positions relative to one another nearly the same as the lines from the centre to the vertices of a regular tetrahedron. Such a configuration of groups of 2-quanta orbits in the carbon atom seems capable of furnishing a suitable foundation for explaining the structure of organic compounds. I shall not discuss this question any further, for it would require a thorough study of the interaction between the motions of the electrons in the atoms forming the molecule. I might mention, however, that the types of molecular models to which we are led are very different from the molecular models which were suggested in my first papers. In these the chemical "valence bonds" were represented by "electron rings" of the same type as those which were assumed to compose the groups of electrons within the individual atoms. It is nevertheless possible to give a general explanation of the chemical properties of the elements without touching on those matters at all. This is largely due to the fact that the structures of combinations of atoms of the same element and of many organic compounds do not have the same significance for our purpose as those molecular structures in which the individual atoms occur as electrically charged ions. The latter kind of compounds, to which the greater number of simple inorganic compounds belong, is frequently called "heteropolar" and possesses a far more typical character than the first compounds which are called "homoeopolar," and whose properties to quite a different degree exhibit the individual peculiarities of the elements. My main purpose will therefore be to consider the fitness which the configurations of the electrons in the various atoms offer for the formation of ions.

Before leaving the carbon atom I should mention, that a model of this atom in which the orbits of the four most lightly bound electrons possess a pronounced tetrahedric symmetry had already been suggested by Landé. In order to agree with the measurements of the size of the atoms he also assumed that these electrons moved in 2_1 orbits. There is, however, this difference between Landé's view and that given here, that while Landé deduced the characteristic properties of the carbon atom solely from an investigation of the simplest form of motion which four electrons can execute employing spatial symmetry, our view originates from a consideration of the stability of the whole atom. For our assumptions about the orbits of the electrons are based directly on an investigation of the interaction between these electrons and the first two bound electrons. The result is that our model of the carbon atom has dynamic properties which are essentially different from the properties of Landé's model.

In order to account for the properties of *the elements in the second half of the second period* it will first of all be necessary to show why the configuration of ten electrons occurring in the neutral atom of neon possesses such a remarkable degree of stability. Previously it has been assumed that the properties of this configuration were due to the interaction between eight electrons which moved in equivalent orbits outside the nucleus and an inner group of two electrons like that in the helium atom. It will be seen, however, that the solution must be sought in an entirely different direction. It cannot be expected that *the 7th electron* will be bound in a 2_1 orbit equivalent to the orbits of the four preceding electrons. The occurrence of five such orbits would so definitely destroy the symmetry in the interaction of these electrons that it is inconceivable that a process resulting in the accession of a fifth electron to this group would be in agreement with the correspondence principle. On the contrary it will be necessary to assume that the four electrons in their exceptionally symmetrical orbital configuration will keep out later captured electrons with the result that these electrons will be bound in orbits of other types.

The orbits which come into consideration for the 7th electron in the nitrogen atom and the 7th, 8th, 9th and 10th electrons in the atoms of the immediately following elements will be circular orbits of the type 2_2. The diameters of these orbits are considerably larger than those of the l_1 orbits of the first two electrons; on the other hand the outermost part of the eccentric 2_1 orbits will extend some distance beyond these circular 2_2 orbits. I shall not here discuss the capture and binding of these electrons. This requires a further investigation of the interaction between the motions of the electrons in the two types of 2-quanta orbits. I shall simply mention, that in the atom of neon in which we will assume that there are four electrons in 2_2 orbits the planes of these orbits must be regarded not only as occupying a position relative to one another characterized by a high degree of spatial symmetry, but also as possessing a configuration harmonizing with the four elliptical 2_1 orbits. An interaction of this kind in which the orbital planes do not coincide can be attained only if the configurations in both subgroups exhibit a systematic deviation from tetrahedral symmetry. This will have the result that the electron groups with 2-quanta orbits in the neon atom will have only a single axis of symmetry which must be supposed to coincide with the axis of symmetry of the innermost group of two electrons.

Before leaving the description of the elements within the second period it may be pointed out that the above considerations offer a basis for interpreting that tendency of the neutral atoms of oxygen and fluorine for capturing further electrons which is responsible for the marked electronegative character of these elements. In fact, this tendency may be ascribed to the fact that the orbits of the last captured electrons will find their place within the region, in which the previously captured electrons move in 2_1 orbits. This suggests an explanation of the great difference between the properties of the elements in the latter half of the second period of the periodic system and those of the elements in the first half, in whose atoms there is only a single type of 2-quanta orbits.

Third Period. Sodium—Argon. We shall now consider the structure of atoms of elements in the third period of the periodic system. This brings us immediately 'to the question of *the binding of the* 11*th electron* in the atom. Here we meet conditions which in some respects are analogous to those connected with the binding of the 7th electron. The same type of argument that applied to the carbon atom shows that the symmetry of the configuration in the neon atom would be essentially, if not entirely, destroyed by the addition of another electron in an orbit of the same type as that in which the last captured electrons were bound. Just as in the case of the 3rd and 7th electrons we may therefore expect to meet a new type of orbit for the 11th electron in the atom, and the orbits which present themselves this time are the 3_1 orbits. An electron in such an orbit will for the greater part of the time remain outside the orbits of the first ten electrons. But at certain moments during the revolution it will penetrate not only into the region of the 2-quanta orbits, but like the 2_1 orbits it will penetrate to distances from the nucleus which are smaller than the radii of the 1-quantum orbits of the two electrons first bound. This fact, which has a most important bearing on the stability of the atom, leads to a peculiar result as regards the binding of the 11th electron. In the sodium atom this electron will move in a field which so far as the outer part of the orbit is concerned deviates only very little from that surrounding the nucleus in the hydrogen atom, but the dimensions of this part of the orbit will, nevertheless, be essentially different from the dimensions of the corresponding part of a 3_1 orbit in the hydrogen atom. This arises from the fact, that even though the electron only enters the inner configuration of the first ten electrons for short intervals during its revolution, this part of the orbit will nevertheless exert an essential influence upon the determination of the principal quantum number. This is directly related to the fact that the motion of the electron in the first part of the orbit deviates only a little from the motion which each of the previously bound electrons in 2_1 orbits executes during a complete revolution. The uncertainty which has prevailed in the determination of the quantum numbers for the stationary states corresponding to a spectrum like that of sodium is connected with this. This question has been discussed by several physicists. From a comparison of the spectral terms of the various alkali metals, Roschdestwensky has drawn the conclusion that the normal state does not, as we might be inclined to expect a priori, correspond to a 1_1 orbit as shown in fig. 2 on page 119, but that this state corresponds to a 2_1 orbit. Schrödinger has arrived at a similar result in an attempt to account for the great difference between the S terms and the terms in the P and D series of the alkali spectra. He assumes that the "outer" electron in the states corresponding to the S terms—in contrast to those corresponding to the P and D terms—penetrates partly into the region of the orbits of the inner electrons during the course of its revolution. These investigations contain without doubt important hints, but in reality the conditions must be very different for the different alkali spectra. Instead of a 2_1 orbit as in lithium we must thus assume for the spectrum of sodium not only that the first spectral term in the S series corresponds to a 3_1 orbit, but also, as a more detailed consideration shows, that the first term in the P series corresponds not to a 2_2 orbit as indicated in fig. 2, but to a 3_2 orbit. If the numbers in this figure were correct, it would require among other things that the P terms should be smaller than the hydrogen terms corresponding to the same principal quantum number. This

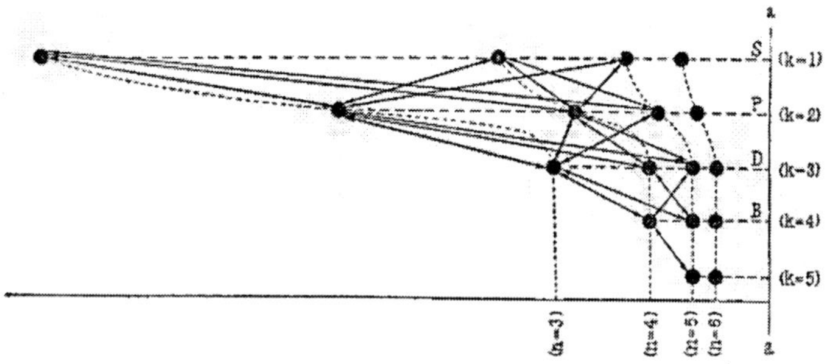

Fig. 3.

would mean that the average effect of the inner electrons could be described as a repulsion greater than would occur if their total electrical charge were united in the nucleus. This, however, cannot be expected from our view of atomic structure. The fact that the last captured electron, at any rate for low values of k, revolves partly inside the orbits of the previously bound electrons will on the contrary involve that the presence of these electrons will give rise to a virtual repulsion which is considerably smaller than that which would be due to their combined charges. Instead of the curves drawn between points in fig. 2 which represent stationary states corresponding to the same value of the principal quantum number running from right to left, we obtain curves which run from left to right, as is indicated in fig. 3. The stationary states are labelled with quantum numbers corresponding to the structure I have described. According to the view underlying fig. 2 the sodium spectrum might be described simply as a distorted hydrogen spectrum, whereas according to fig. 3 there is not only distortion but also complete disappearance of certain terms of low quantum numbers. It may be stated, that this view not only appears to offer an explanation of the magnitude of the terms, but that the complexity of the terms in the P and D series finds a natural explanation in the deviation of the configuration of the ten electrons first bound from a purely central symmetry. This lack of symmetry has its origin in the configuration of the two innermost electrons and "transmits" itself to the outer parts of the atomic structure, since the 2_1 orbits penetrate partly into the region of these electrons.

This view of the sodium spectrum provides at the same time an immediate explanation of the pronounced electropositive properties of sodium, since the last bound electron in the sodium atom is still more loosely bound than the last captured electron in the lithium atom. In this connection it might be mentioned that the increase in atomic volume with increasing atomic number in the family of the alkali metals finds a simple explanation in the successively looser binding of the valency electrons. In his work on the X-ray spectra Sommerfeld at an earlier period regarded this increase in the atomic volumes as supporting the assumption that the principal quantum number of the orbit of the valency electrons increases by unity as we pass from one metal to the next in the family. His later investigations on the series spectra have led him, however, definitely to abandon this assumption. At first sight it might also appear to entail a far greater increase in the atomic volume than that actually observed. A simple explanation of this fact is however afforded by realizing that the orbit of the electron will run partly inside the region of the inner orbit and that therefore the "effective" quantum number which corresponds to the outer almost elliptical loop will be much smaller than the principal quantum number, by which the whole central orbit is described. It may be mentioned that Vegard in his investigations on the X-ray spectra has also proposed the assumption of successively increasing quantum numbers for the electronic orbits in the various groups of the atom, reckoned from the nucleus outward. He has introduced assumptions about the relations between the numbers of electrons in the various groups of the atom and the lengths of the periods in the periodic system which exhibit certain formal similarities with the results presented here. But Vegard's considerations do not offer points of departure for a further consideration of the evolution and stability of the groups, and consequently no basis for a detailed interpretation of the properties of the elements.

When we consider the elements following sodium in the third period of the periodic system we meet in *the binding of the* 12*th,* 13*th and* 14*th electrons* conditions which are analogous to those we met in the binding of the 4th, 5th and 6th electrons. In the elements of the third periods, however, we possess a far more detailed knowledge of the series spectra. Too little is known about the beryllium spectrum to draw conclusions about the binding of the fourth electron, but we may infer directly from the well-known arc spectrum of magnesium that the 12th electron in the atom of this element is bound in a 3_1 orbit. As regards the binding of the 13th electron we meet in aluminium an absorption spectrum different in structure to that of the alkali metals. In fact here not the lines of the principal series but the lines of the sharp and diffuse series are absorption lines. Consequently it is the first member of the P terms and not of the S terms which corresponds to the normal state of the aluminium atom, and we must assume that the 13th electron is bound in a 3_2 orbit. This, however, would hardly seem to be a general property of the binding of the 13th electron in atoms, but rather to arise from the special conditions for the binding of the last electron in an atom, where already there are two other electrons bound as loosely as the valency electron of aluminium. At the present state of the theory it seems best to assume that in the silicon atom the four last captured electrons will move in 3_1 orbits forming a configuration possessing symmetrical properties similar to the outer configuration of the four electrons in 2_1 orbits in carbon. Like what we assumed for the latter configuration we shall expect that the configuration of the 3_1 orbits occurring for the first time in silicon possesses such a completion, that the addition of a further electron in a 3_1 orbit to the atom of the following elements is impossible, and that *the* 15*th electron* in the elements of higher atomic number will be bound in a new type of orbit. In this case, however, the orbits with which we meet will not be circular, as in the capture of the 7th electron, but will be rotating eccentric orbits of the type 3_2. This is very closely related to the fact, mentioned above, that the non-circular orbits will correspond to a firmer binding than the circular orbits having the same value for the principal quantum number, since the electrons will at certain moments penetrate much farther into the interior of the atom. Even though a 3_2 orbit will not penetrate into the innermost configuration of 1_1 orbits, it will penetrate to distances from the nucleus which are considerably less than the radii of the circular 22 orbits. In the case of the 16th, 17th and 18th electrons the conditions are similar to those for the 15th. So for argon we may expect a configuration in which the ten innermost electrons move in orbits of the same type as in the neon atom while the last eight electrons will form a configuration of four 3_1 orbits and four 3_2 orbits, whose symmetrical properties must be regarded as closely corresponding to the configuration of 2-quanta orbits in the neon atom. At the same time, as this picture suggests a qualitative explanation of the similarity of the chemical properties of the elements in the latter part of the second and third periods, it also opens up the possibility of a natural explanation of the conspicuous difference from a quantitative aspect.

Fourth Period. Potassium—Krypton. In the fourth period we meet at first elements which resemble chemically those at the beginning of the two previous periods. This is also what we should expect. We must thus assume that *the* 19*th electron* is bound in a new type of orbit, and a closer consideration shows that this will be a 4_1 orbit. The points which were emphasized in connection with the binding of the last electron in the sodium atom will be even more marked here on account of the larger quantum number by which the orbits of the inner electrons are characterized. In fact, in the potassium atom the 4_1 orbit of the 19th electron will, as far as inner loops are concerned, coincide closely with the shape of a 3_1 orbit. On this account, therefore, the dimensions of the outer part of the orbit will not only deviate greatly from the dimensions of a 4_1 orbit in the hydrogen atom, but will coincide closely with a hydrogen orbit of the type 2_1, the dimensions of which are about four times smaller than the 4_1 hydrogen orbit. This result allows an immediate explanation of the main features of the chemical properties and the spectrum of potassium. Corresponding results apply to calcium, in the neutral atom of which there will be two valency electrons in equivalent 4_1 orbits.

After calcium the properties of the elements in the fourth

period of the periodic system deviate, however, more and more from the corresponding elements in the previous periods, until in the family of the iron metals we meet elements whose properties are essentially different. Proceeding to still higher atomic numbers we again meet different conditions. Thus we find in the latter part of the fourth period a series of elements whose chemical properties approach more and more to the properties of the elements at the end of the preceding periods, until finally with atomic number 36 we again meet one of the inactive gases, namely krypton. This is exactly what we should expect. The formation and stability of the atoms of the elements in the first three periods require that each of the first 18 electrons in the atom shall be bound in each succeeding element in an orbit of the same principal quantum number as that possessed by the particular electron, when it first appeared. It is readily seen that this is no longer the case for the 19th electron. With increasing nuclear charge and the consequent decrease in the difference between the fields of force inside and outside the region of the orbits of the first 18 bound electrons, the dimensions of those parts of a 4_1 orbit which fall outside will approach more and more to the dimensions of a 4-quantum orbit calculated on the assumption that the interaction between the electrons in the atom may be neglected. *With increasing atomic number a point will therefore be reached where a 3_3 orbit will correspond to a firmer binding of the 19th electron than a 4_1 orbit*, and this occurs as early as at the beginning of the fourth period. This cannot only be anticipated from a simple calculation but is confirmed in a striking way from an examination of the series spectra. While the spectrum of potassium indicates that the 4_1 orbit corresponds to a binding which is more than twice as firm as in a 3_3 orbit corresponding to the first spectral term in the D series, the conditions are entirely different as soon as calcium is reached. We shall not consider the arc spectrum which is emitted during the capture of the 20th electron but the spark spectrum which corresponds to the capture and binding of the 19th electron. While the spark spectrum of magnesium exhibits great similarity with the sodium spectrum as regards the values of the spectral terms in the various series—apart from the fact that the constant appearing in formula (12) is four times as large as the Rydberg constant—we meet in the spark spectrum of calcium the remarkable condition that the first term of the D series is larger than the first term of the P series and is only a little smaller than the first term of the S series, which may be regarded as corresponding to the binding of the 19th electron in the normal state of the calcium atom. These facts are shown in figure 4 which gives a survey of the stationary states corresponding to the arc spectra of sodium and potassium. As in figures 2 and 3 of the sodium spectrum, we have disregarded the complexity of the spectral terms, and the numbers characterizing the stationary states are simply the quantum numbers n and k. For the sake of comparison the scale in which the energy of the different states is indicated is chosen four times as small for the spark spectra as for the arc spectra. Consequently the vertical lines indicated

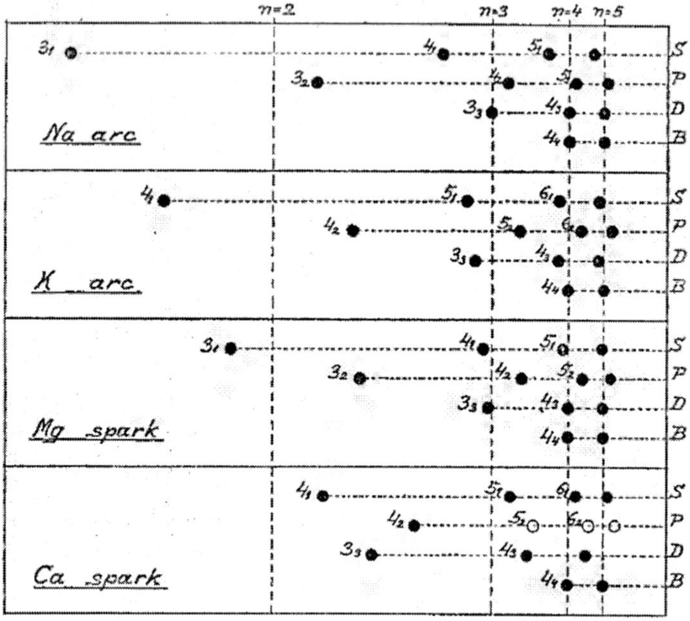

Fig. 4.

with various values of n correspond for the arc spectra to the spectral terms of hydrogen, for the spark spectra to the terms of the helium spectrum given by formula (7). Comparing the change in the relative firmness in the binding of the 19th electron in a 4_1 and 3_3 orbit for potassium and calcium we see that we must be prepared already for the next element, scandium, to find that the 3_3 orbit will correspond to a stronger binding of this electron than a 4_1 orbit. On the other hand it follows from previous remarks that the binding will be much lighter than for the first 18 electrons which agrees that in chemical combinations scandium appears electropositively with three valencies.

If we proceed to the following elements, a still larger number of 3_3 orbits will occur in the normal state of these atoms, since the number of such electron orbits will depend upon the firmness of their binding compared to the firmness with which an electron is bound in a 4_1 orbit, in which type of orbit at least the last captured electron in the atom may be assumed to move. We therefore meet conditions which are essentially different from those which we have considered in connection with the previous periods, so that here we have to do with *the successive development of one of the inner groups of electrons in the atom*, in this case with groups of electrons in 3-quanta orbits. Only when the development of this group has been completed may we expect to find once more a corresponding change in the properties of the elements with increasing atomic number such as we find in the preceding periods. The properties of the elements in the latter part of the fourth period show immediately that the group, when completed, will possess 18 electrons. Thus in krypton, for example, we may expect besides the groups of 1, 2 and 3-quanta orbits a markedly symmetrical configuration of 8 electrons in 4-quanta orbits consisting of four 4_1 orbits and four 4_2 orbits.

The question now arises: In which way will the gradual formation of the group of electrons having 3-quanta orbits take place? From analogy with the constitution of the groups of electrons with 2-quanta orbits we might at first sight be inclined to suppose that the complete group of 3-quanta orbits would consist of three subgroups of four electrons each in orbits of the types 3_1, 3_2 and 3_3 respectively, so that the total number of electrons would be 12 instead of 18. Further consideration shows, however, that such an expectation would not be justified. The stability of the configuration of eight electrons with 2-quanta orbits occurring in neon must be ascribed not only to the symmetrical configuration of the electronic orbits in the two subgroups of 2_1 and 2_2 orbits respectively, but fully as much to the possibility of bringing the orbits inside these subgroups into harmonic relation with one another. The situation is different, however, for the groups of electrons with 3-quanta orbits. Three subgroups of four orbits each cannot in this case be expected to come into interaction with one another in a correspondingly simple manner. On the contrary we must assume that the presence of electrons in 3_3 orbits will diminish the harmony of the orbits within the first two 3-quanta subgroups, at any rate when a point is reached where the 19th electron is no longer, as was the case with scandium, bound considerably more lightly than the previously bound electrons in 3-quanta orbits, but has been drawn so far into the atom that it revolves within essentially the same region of the atom where these electrons move. We shall now assume that this decrease in the harmony will so to say "open" the previously "closed" configuration of electrons in orbits of these types. As regards the final result, the number 18 indicates that after the group is finally formed there will be three subgroups containing six electrons each. Even if it has not at present been possible to follow in detail the various steps in the formation of the group this result is nevertheless confirmed in an interesting manner by the fact that it is possible to arrange three configurations having six electrons each in a simple manner relative to one another. The configuration of the subgroups does not exhibit a tetrahedral symmetry like the groups of 2-quanta orbits in carbon, but a symmetry which, so far as the relative orientation of the normals to the planes of the orbits is concerned, may be described as trigonal.

In spite of the great difference in the properties of the elements of this period, compared with those of the preceding period, the completion of the group of 18 electrons in 3-quanta orbits in the fourth period may to a certain extent be said to have the same characteristic results as the completion of the group of 2-quanta orbits in the second period. As we have seen, this determined not only the properties of neon as an inactive gas, but in addition the electronegative properties of the preceding elements and the electropositive properties of the elements which follow. The fact that there is no inactive gas possessing an outer group of 18 electrons is very easily accounted for by the much larger dimensions which a 3_3 orbit has in comparison with a 2_2 orbit revolving in the same field of force. On this account a complete 3-quanta group cannot occur as the outermost group in a neutral atom, but only in positively charged ions. The characteristic decrease in valency which we meet in copper, shown by the appearance of the singly charged cuprous ions, indicates the same tendency towards the completion of a symmetrical configuration of electrons that we found in the marked electronegative character of an element like fluorine. Direct evidence that a complete group of 3-quanta orbits is present in the cuprous ion is given by the spectrum of copper which, in contrast to the extremely complicated spectra of the preceding elements resulting from the unsymmetrical character of the inner system, possesses a simple structure very much like that of the sodium spectrum. This may no doubt be ascribed to a simple symmetrical structure present in the cuprous ion similar to that in the sodium ion, although the great difference in the constitution of the outer group of electrons in these ions is shown both by the considerable difference in the values of the spectral terms and in the separation of the doublets in the P terms of the two spectra. The occurrence of the cupric compounds shows, however, that the firmness of binding in the group of 3-quanta orbits in the copper atom is not as great as the firmness with which the electrons are bound in the group of 2-quanta orbits in the sodium atom. Zinc, which is always divalent, is the first element in which the groups of the electrons are so firmly bound that they cannot be removed by ordinary chemical processes.

The picture I have given of the formation and structure of the atoms of the elements in the fourth period gives an explanation of the chemical and spectral properties. In addition it is supported by evidence of a different nature to that which we have hitherto used. It is a familiar fact, that the elements in the fourth period differ markedly from the elements in the preceding periods partly in their *magnetic properties* and partly in the *characteristic colours* of their compounds. Paramagnetism and colours do occur in elements belonging to the foregoing periods, but not in simple compounds where the atoms considered enter as ions. Many elements of the fourth period, on the contrary, exhibit paramagnetic properties and characteristic colours even in dissociated aqueous solutions. The importance of this has been emphasized by Ladenburg in his attempt to explain the properties of the elements in the long periods of the periodic system (see page 111). Langmuir in order to account for the difference between the fourth period and the preceding periods simply assumed that the atom, in addition to the layers of cells containing 8 electrons each, possesses an outer layer of cells with room for 18 electrons which is completely filled for the first time in the case of krypton. Ladenburg, on the other hand, assumes that for some reason or other an intermediate layer is developed between the inner electronic configuration in the atom appearing already in argon, and the external group of valency electrons. This layer commences with scandium and is completed exactly at the end of the family of iron metals. In support of this assumption Ladenburg not only mentions the chemical properties of the elements in the fourth period, but also refers to the paramagnetism and colours which occur exactly in the elements, where this intermediate layer should be in development. It is seen that Ladenburg's ideas exhibit certain formal similarities with the interpretation I have given above of the appearance of the fourth period, and it is interesting to note that our view, based on a direct investigation of the conditions for the formation of the atoms, enables us to understand the relation emphasized by Ladenburg.

Our ordinary electrodynamic conceptions are probably insufficient to form a basis for an explanation of atomic magnetism. This is hardly to be wondered at when we remember that they have not proved adequate to account for the phenomena of radiation which are connected with the intimate interaction between the electric and magnetic forces arising from the motion of the electrons. In whatever way these difficulties may be solved it seems simplest to assume that the occurrence of magnetism, such as we meet in the elements of the fourth period, results from a lack of symmetry in the internal structure of the atom, thus preventing the magnetic forces arising from the motion of the electrons from forming a system of closed lines of force running wholly within the atom. While it has been assumed that the ions of the elements in the previous periods, whether positively or negatively charged, contain configurations of marked symmetrical character, we must, however, be prepared to encounter a definite lack of symmetry in the electronic configurations in ions of those elements within the fourth period which contain a group of electrons in 3-quanta orbits in the transition stage between symmetrical configurations of 8 and 18 electrons respectively. As pointed out by Kossel, the experimental results exhibit an extreme simplicity, the magnetic moment of the ions depending only on the number of electrons in the ion. Ferric ions, for example, exhibit the same atomic magnetism as manganous ions, while manganic ions exhibit the same atomic magnetism as chromous ions. It is in beautiful agreement with what we have assumed about the structure of the atoms of copper and zinc, that the magnetism disappears with those ions containing 28 electrons which, as I stated, must be assumed to contain a complete group of 3-quanta orbits. On the whole a consideration of the magnetic properties of the elements within the fourth period gives us a vivid impression of how a wound in the otherwise symmetrical inner structure is first developed and then healed as we pass from element to element. It is to be hoped that a further investigation of the magnetic properties will give us a clue to the way in which the group of electrons in 3-quanta orbits is developed step by step.

Also the colours of the ions directly support our view of atomic structure. According to the postulates of the quantum theory absorption as well as emission of radiation is regarded as taking place during transitions between stationary states. The occurrence of colours, that is to say the absorption of light in the visible region of the spectrum, is evidence of transitions involving energy changes of the same order of magnitude as those giving the usual optical spectra of the elements. In contrast to the ions of the elements of the preceding periods where all the electrons are assumed to be very firmly bound, the occurrence of such processes in the fourth period is exactly what we should expect. For the development and completion of the electronic groups with 3-quanta orbits will proceed, so to say, in competition with the binding of electrons in orbits of higher quanta, since the binding of electrons in 3-quanta orbits occurs when the electrons in these orbits are bound more firmly than electrons in 4_1 orbits. The development of the group will therefore proceed to the point where we may say there is equilibrium between the two kinds of orbits. This condition may be assumed to be intimately connected not only with the colour of the ions, but also with the tendency of the elements to form ions with different valencies. This is in contrast to the elements of the first periods where the charge of the ions in aqueous solutions is always the same for one and the same element.

Fifth Period. Rubidium—Xenon. The structure of the atoms in the remaining periods may be followed up in complete analogy with what has already been said. Thus we shall assume that the 37th and 38th electrons in the elements of the fifth period are bound in 5_1 orbits. This is supported by the measurements of the arc spectrum of rubidium and the spark spectrum of strontium. The latter spectrum indicates at the same time that 4_3 orbits will soon appear, and therefore in this period, which like the 4th contains 18 elements, we must assume that we are witnessing a *further stage in the development of the electronic group of* 4-*quanta* *orbits.* The first stage in the formation of this group may be said to have been attained in krypton with the appearance of a symmetrical configuration of eight electrons consisting of two subgroups each of four electrons in 4_1 and 4_2 orbits. A second preliminary completion must be regarded as having been reached with the appearance of a symmetrical configuration of 18 electrons in the case of silver, consisting of three subgroups with six electrons each in orbits of the types 4_1, 4_2 and 4_3. Everything that has been said about the successive formation of the group of electrons with 3-quanta orbits applies unchanged to this stage in the transformation of the group with 4-quanta orbits. For in no case have we made use of the absolute values of the quantum numbers nor of assumptions concerning the form of the orbits but only of the number of possible types of orbits which might come into consideration. At the same time it may be of interest to mention that the properties of these elements compared with those of the foregoing period nevertheless show a difference corresponding exactly to what would be expected from the difference in the types of orbits. For instance, the divergencies from the characteristic valency conditions of the elements in the second and third periods appear later in the fifth period than for elements in the fourth period. While an element like titanium in the fourth period already shows a marked tendency to occur with various valencies, on the other hand an element like zirconium is still quadri-valent like carbon in the second period and silicon in the third. A simple investigation of the kinematic properties of the orbits of the electrons shows in fact that an electron in an eccentric 4_3 orbit of an element in the fifth period will be considerably more loosely bound than an electron in a circular 3_3 orbit of the corresponding element in the fourth period, while electrons which are bound in eccentric orbits of the types 5_1 and 4_1 respectively will correspond to a binding of about the same firmness.

At the end of the fifth period we may assume that xenon, the atomic number of which is 54, has a structure which in addition to the two 1-quantum, eight 2-quanta, eighteen 3-quanta and eighteen 4-quanta orbits already mentioned contains a symmetrical configuration of eight electrons in 5-quanta orbits consisting of two subgroups with four electrons each in 5_1 and 5_2 orbits respectively.

Sixth Period. Caesium—Niton. If we now consider the atoms of elements of still higher atomic number, we must first of all assume that the 55th and 56th electrons in the atoms of caesium and barium are bound in 6_1 orbits. This is confirmed by the spectra of these elements. It is clear, however, that we must be prepared shortly to meet entirely new conditions. With increasing nuclear charge we shall have to expect not only that an electron in a 5_3 orbit will be bound more firmly than in a 6_1 orbit, but we must also expect that a moment will arrive when during the formation of the atom a 4_4 orbit will represent a firmer binding of the electron than an orbit of 5 or 6-quanta, in much the same way as in the elements of the fourth period a new stage in the development of the 3-quanta group was started when a point was reached where for the first time the 19th electron was bound in a 3_3 orbit instead of in a 4_1 orbit. We shall thus expect in the sixth period to meet with a new stage in the development of the group with 4-quanta orbits. Once this point has been reached we must be prepared to find with increasing atomic number a number of elements following one another, which as in the family of the iron metals have very nearly the same properties. The similarity will, however, be still more pronounced, since in this case we are concerned with the successive transformation of a configuration of electrons which lies deeper in the interior of the atom. You will have already guessed that what I have in view is a simple explanation of the occurrence of the *family of rare earths* at the beginning of the sixth period. As in the case of the transformation and completion of the group of 3-quanta orbits in the fourth period and the partial completion of groups of 4-quanta orbits in the fifth period, we may immediately deduce from the length of the sixth period the number of electrons, namely 32, which are finally contained in the 4-quanta group of orbits. Analogous to what applied to the group of 3-quanta orbits it is probable that, when the group is completed, it will contain eight electrons in each of the four subgroups. Even though it has not yet been possible to follow the development of the group step by step, we can even here give some theoretical evidence in favour of the occurrence of a symmetrical configuration of exactly this number of electrons. I shall simply mention that it is not possible without coincidence of the planes of the orbits to arrive at an interaction between four subgroups of six electrons each in a configuration of simple trigonal symmetry, which is equally simple as that shown by three subgroups. The difficulties which we meet make it probable that a harmonic interaction can be attained precisely by four groups each containing eight electrons the orbital configurations of which exhibit axial symmetry.

Just as in the case of the family of the iron metals in the fourth period, the proposed explanation of the occurrence of the family of rare earths in the sixth period is supported in an interesting manner by an investigation of the magnetic properties of these elements. In spite of the great chemical similarity the members of this family exhibit very different magnetic properties, so that while some of them exhibit but very little magnetism others exhibit a greater magnetic moment per atom than any other element which has been investigated. It is also possible to give a simple interpretation of the peculiar colours exhibited by the compounds of these elements in much the same way as in the case of the family of iron metals in the fourth period. The idea that the appearance of the group of the rare earths is connected with the development of inner groups in the atom is not in itself new and has for instance been considered by Vegard in connection with his work on X-ray spectra. The new feature of the present considerations lies, however, in the emphasis laid on the peculiar way in which the relative strength of the binding for two orbits of the same principal quantum number but of different shapes varies with the nuclear charge and with the number of electrons previously bound. Due to this fact the presence of a group like that of the rare earths in the sixth period may be considered as a direct consequence of the theory and might actually have been predicted on a quantum theory, adapted to the explanation of the properties of the elements within the preceding periods in the way I have shown.

Besides *the final development of the group of* 4-*quanta orbits* we observe in the sixth period in the family of the platinum metals *the second stage in the development of the group of* 5-*quanta orbits.* Also in the radioactive, chemically inactive gas niton, which completes this period, we observe the first preliminary step in the development of a group of electrons with 6-quanta orbits. In the atom of this element, in addition to the groups of electrons of two 1-quantum, eight 2-quanta, eighteen 3-quanta, thirty-two 4-quanta and eighteen 5-quanta orbits respectively, there is also an outer symmetrical configuration of eight electrons in 6-quanta orbits, which we shall assume to consist of two subgroups with four electrons each in 6_1 and 6_2 orbits respectively.

Seventh Period. In the seventh and last period of the periodic system we may expect the appearance of 7-quanta orbits in the normal state of the atom. Thus in the neutral atom of radium in addition to the electronic structure of niton there will be two electrons in 7_1 orbits which will penetrate during their revolution not only into the region of the orbits of electrons possessing lower values for the principal quantum number, but even to distances from the nucleus which are less than the radii of the orbits of the innermost 1-quantum orbits. The properties of the elements in the seventh period are very similar to the properties of the elements in the fifth period. Thus, in contrast to the conditions in the sixth period, there are no elements whose properties resemble one another like those of the rare earths. In exact analogy with what has already been said about the relations between the properties of the elements in the fourth and fifth periods this may be very simply explained by the fact that an eccentric 5_4 orbit will correspond to a considerably looser binding of an electron in the atom of an element of the seventh period than the binding of an electron in a circular 4_4 orbit in the corresponding element of the sixth period, while there will be a much smaller difference in the firmness of the binding of these electrons in orbits of the types 7_1 and 6_1 respectively.

It is well known that the seventh period is not complete, for no atom has been found having an atomic number greater than 92. This is probably connected with the fact that the last elements in the system are radioactive and that nuclei of atoms with a total charge greater than 92 will not be sufficiently stable to exist under conditions where the elements can be observed. It is tempting to sketch a picture of the atoms formed by the capture and binding of electrons around nuclei having higher charges, and thus to obtain some idea of the properties which the corresponding hypothetical elements might be expected to exhibit. I shall not develop this matter further, however, since the general results we should get will be evident to you from the views I have developed to explain the properties of the elements actually observed. A survey of these results is given in the following table, which gives a symbolical representation of the atomic structure of the inactive gases which complete the first six periods in the periodic system. In order to emphasize the progressive change the table includes the probable arrangement of electrons in the next atom which would possess properties like the inactive gases.

The view of atomic constitution underlying this table, which involves configurations of electrons moving with large velocities between each other, so that the electrons in the "outer" groups penetrate into the region of the orbits of the electrons of the "inner" groups, is of course completely different from such statical models of the atom as are proposed by Langmuir. But quite apart from this it will be seen that the arrangement of the electronic groups in the atom, to which we have been lead by tracing the way in which each single electron has been bound, is essentially different from the arrangement of the groups in Langmuir's theory. In order to explain the properties of the elements of the sixth period Langmuir assumes for instance that, in addition to the inner layers of cells containing 2, 8, 8, 18 and 18 electrons respectively, which are employed to account for the properties of the elements in the earlier periods, the atom also possesses a layer of cells with room for 32 electrons which is just completed in the case of niton.

Element	Atomic number	Number of Electrons in n_k-orbits																							
		1_1	2_1	2_2	3_1	3_2	3_3	4_1	4_2	4_3	4_4	5_1	5_2	5_3	5_4	5_5	6_1	6_2	6_3	6_4	6_5	6_6	7_1	7_2	7_3
Helium	2	2																							
Neon	10	2	4	4																					
Argon	18	2	4	4	4	4	–																		
Krypton	36	2	4	4	6	6	6	4	4	–	–														
Xenon	54	2	4	4	6	6	6	6	6	6	–	4	4	–	–	–									
Niton	86	2	4	4	6	6	6	8	8	8	8	6	6	6	–	–	4	4	–	–	–	–			
?	118	2	4	4	6	6	6	8	8	8	8	8	8	8	8	–	6	6	6	–	–	–	4	4	–

In this connection it may be of interest to mention a recent paper by Bury, to which my attention was first drawn after the deliverance of this address, and which contains an interesting survey of the chemical properties of the elements based on similar conceptions of atomic structure as those applied by Lewis and Langmuir. From purely chemical considerations Bury arrives at conclusions which as regards the arrangement and completion of the groups in the main coincide with those of the present theory, the outlines of which were given in my letters to Nature mentioned in the introduction.

Survey of the periodic table. The results given in this address are also illustrated by means of the representation of the periodic system given in fig. 1. In this figure the frames are meant to indicate such elements in which one of the "inner" groups is in a stage of development. Thus there will be found in the fourth and fifth periods a single frame indicating the final completion of the electronic group with 3-quanta orbits, and the last stage but one in the development of the group with 4-quanta orbits respectively. In the sixth period it has been necessary to introduce two frames, of which the inner one indicates the last stage of the evolution of the group with 4-quanta orbits, giving rise to the rare earths. This occurs at a place in the periodic system where the third stage in the development of an electronic group with 5-quanta orbits, indicated by the outer frame, has already begun. In this connection it will be seen that the inner frame encloses a smaller number of elements than is usually attributed to the family of the rare earths. At the end of this group an uncertainty exists, due to the fact that no element of atomic number 72 is known with certainty. However, as indicated in fig. 1, we must conclude from the theory that the group with 4-quanta orbits is finally completed in lutetium (71). This element therefore ought to be the last in the sequence of consecutive elements with similar properties in the first half of the sixth period, and at the place 72 an element must be expected which in its chemical and physical properties is homologous with zirconium and thorium. This, which is already indited on Julius Thomsen's old table, has also been pointed out by Bury. [Quite recently Dauvillier has in an investigation of the X-ray spectrum excited in preparations containing rare earths, observed certain faint lines which he ascribes to an element of atomic number 72. This element is identified by him as the element celtium, belonging to the family of rare earths, the existence of which had previously been suspected by Urbain. Quite apart from the difficulties which this result, if correct, might entail for atomic theories, it would, since the rare earths according to chemical view possess three valencies, imply a rise in positive valency of two units when passing from the element 72 to the next element 73, tantalum. This would mean an exception from the otherwise general rule, that the valency never increases by more than one unit when passing from one element to the next in the periodic table.] In the case of the incomplete seventh period the full drawn frame indicates the third stage in the development of the electronic group with 6-quanta orbits, which must begin in actinium. The dotted frame indicates the last stage but one in the development of the group with 5-quanta orbits, which hitherto has not been observed, but which ought to begin shortly after uranium, if it has not already begun in this element.

With reference to the homology of the elements the exceptional position of the elements enclosed by frames in fig. 1 is further emphasized by taking care that, in spite of the large similarity many elements exhibit, no connecting lines are drawn between two elements which occupy different positions in the system with respect to framing. In fact, the large chemical similarity between, for instance, aluminium and scandium, both of which are trivalent and pronounced electropositive elements, is directly or indirectly emphasized in the current representations of the periodic table. While this procedure is justified by the analogous structure of the trivalent ions of these elements, our more detailed ideas of atomic structure suggest, however, marked differences in the physical properties of aluminium and scandium, originating in the essentially different character of the way in which the last three electrons in the neutral atom are bound. This fact gives probably a direct explanation of the marked difference existing between the spectra of aluminium and scandium. Even if the spectrum of scandium is not yet sufficiently cleared up, this difference seems to be of a much more fundamental character than for instance the difference between the arc spectra of sodium and copper, which apart from the large difference in the absolute values of the spectral terms possess a completely analogous structure, as previously mentioned in this essay. On the whole we must expect that the spectra of elements in the later periods lying inside a frame will show new features compared with the spectra of the elements in the first three periods. This expectation seems supported by recent work on the spectrum of manganese by Catalan, which appeared just before the printing of this essay.

Before I leave the interpretation of the chemical properties by means of this atomic model I should like to remind you once again of the fundamental principles which we have used. The whole theory has evolved from an investigation of the way in which electrons can be captured by an atom. The formation of an atom was held to consist in the successive binding of electrons, this binding resulting in radiation according to the quantum theory. According to the fundamental postulates of the theory this binding takes place in stages by transitions between stationary states accompanied by emission of radiation. For the problem of the stability of the atom the essential problem is at what stage such a process comes to an end. As regards this point the postulates give no direct information, but here the correspondence principle is brought in. Even though it has been possible to penetrate considerably further at many points than the time has permitted me to indicate to you, still it has not yet been possible to follow in detail all stages in the formation of the atoms. We cannot say, for instance, that the above table of the atomic constitution of the inert gases may in every detail be considered as the unambiguous result of applying the correspondence principle. On the other hand it appears that our considerations already place the empirical data in a light which scarcely permits of an essentially different interpretation of the properties of the elements based upon the postulates of the quantum theory. This applies not only to the series spectra and the close relationship of these to the chemical properties of the elements, but also to the X-ray spectra, the consideration of which leads us into an investigation of interatomic processes of an entirely different character. As we have already mentioned, it is necessary to assume that the emission of the latter spectra is connected with processes which may be described as a reorganization of the completely formed atom after a disturbance produced in the interior of the atom by the action of external forces.

IV. REORGANIZATION OF ATOMS AND X-RAY SPECTRA

As in the case of the series spectra it has also been possible to represent the frequency of each line in the X-ray spectrum of an element as the difference of two of a set of spectral terms. We shall therefore assume that each X-ray line is due to a transition between two stationary states of the atom. The values of the atomic energy corresponding to these states are frequently referred to as the "energy levels" of the X-ray spectra. The great difference between the origin of the X-ray and the series spectra is clearly seen, however, in the difference of the laws applying to the absorption of radiation in the X-ray and the optical regions of the spectra. The absorption by non-excited atoms in the latter case is connected with those lines in the series spectrum which correspond to combinations of the various spectral terms with the largest of these terms. As has been shown, especially by the investigations of Wagner and de Broglie, the absorption in the X-ray region, on the other hand, is connected not with the X-ray lines but with certain spectral regions commencing at the so-called "absorption edges." The frequencies of these edges agree very closely with the spectral terms used to account for the X-ray lines. We shall now see how the conception of atomic structure developed in the preceding pages offers a simple interpretation of these facts. Let us consider the following question: What changes in the state of the atom can be produced by the absorption of radiation, and which processes of emission can be initiated by such changes?

Absorption and emission of X-rays and correspondence principle. The possibility of producing a change at all in the motion of an electron in the interior of an atom by means of radiation must in the first place be regarded as intimately connected with the character of the interaction between the electrons within the separate groups. In contrast to the forms of motion where at every moment the position of the electrons exhibits polygonal or polyhedral symmetry, the conception of this interaction evolved from a consideration of the possible formation of atoms by successive binding of electrons has such a character that the harmonic components in the motion of an electron are in general represented in the resulting electric moment of the atom. As a result of this it will be possible to release a single electron from the interaction with the other electrons in the same group by a process which possesses the necessary analogy with an absorption process on the ordinary electrodynamic view claimed by the correspondence principle. The points of view on which we based the interpretation of the development and completion of the groups during the formation of an atom imply, on the other hand, that just as no additional electron can be taken up into a previously completed group in the atom by a change involving emission of radiation, similarly it will not be possible for a new electron to be added to such a group, when the state of the atom is changed by absorption of radiation. This means that an electron which belongs to one of the inner groups of the atom, as a consequence of an absorption process—besides the case where it leaves the atom completely—can only go over either to an incompleted group, or to an orbit where the electron during the greater part of its revolution moves at a distance from the nucleus large compared to the distance of the other electrons. On account of the peculiar conditions of stability which control the occurrence of incomplete groups in the interior of the atom, the energy which is necessary to bring about a transition to such a group will in general differ very little from that required to remove the particular electron completely from the atom. We must therefore assume that the energy levels corresponding to the absorption edges indicate to a first approximation the amount of work that is required to remove an electron in one of the inner groups completely from the atom. The correspondence principle also provides a basis for understanding the experimental evidence about the appearance of the emission lines of the X-ray spectra due to transitions between the stationary states corresponding to these energy levels. Thus the nature of the interaction between the electrons in the groups of the atom implies that each electron in the atom is so to say prepared, independently of the other electrons in the same group, to seize any opportunity which is offered to become more firmly bound by being taken up into a group of electrons with orbits corresponding to smaller values of the principal quantum number. It is evident, however, that on the basis of our views of atomic structure, such an opportunity is always at hand as soon as an electron has been removed from one of these groups.

At the same time that our view of the atom leads to a natural conception of the phenomena of emission and absorption of X-rays, agreeing closely with that by which Kossel has attempted to give a formal explanation of the experimental observations, it also suggests a simple explanation of those quantitative relations holding for the frequencies of the lines which have been discovered by Moseley and Sommerfeld. These researches brought to light a remarkable and far-reaching similarity between the Röntgen spectrum of a given element and the spectrum which would be expected to appear upon the binding of a single electron by the nucleus. This similarity we immediately understand if we recall that in the normal state of the atom there are electrons moving in orbits which, with certain limitations, correspond to all stages of such a binding process and that, when an electron is removed from its original place in the atom, processes may be started within the atom which will correspond to all transitions between these stages permitted by the correspondence principle. This brings us at once out of those difficulties which apparently arise, when one attempts to account for the origin of the X-ray spectra by means of an atomic structure, suited to explain the periodic system. This difficulty has been felt to such an extent that it has led Sommerfeld for example in his recent work to assume that the configurations of the electrons in the various atoms of one and the same element may be different even under usual conditions. Since, in contrast to our ideas, he supposed all electrons in the principal groups of the atom to move in equivalent orbits, he is compelled to assume that these groups are different in the different atoms, corresponding to different possible types of orbital shapes. Such an assumption, however, seems inconsistent with an interpretation of the definite character of the physical and chemical properties of the elements, and stands in marked contradiction with the points of view about the stability of the atoms which form the basis of the view of atomic structure here proposed.

X-ray spectra and atomic structure. In this connection it is of interest to emphasize that the group distribution of the electrons in the atom, on which we have based both the explanation of the periodic system and the classification of the lines in the X-ray spectra, shows itself in an entirely different manner in these two phenomena. While the characteristic change of the chemical properties with atomic number is due to the gradual development and completion of the groups of the loosest bound electrons, the characteristic absence of almost every trace of a periodic change in the X-ray spectra is due to two causes. Firstly the electronic configuration of the completed groups is repeated unchanged for increasing atomic number, and secondly the gradual way in which the incompleted groups are developed implies that a type of orbit, from the moment when it for the first time appears in the normal state of the neutral atom, always will occur in this state and will correspond to a steadily increasing firmness of binding. The development of the groups in the atom with increasing atomic number, which governs the chemical properties of the elements shows itself in the X-ray spectra mainly in the appearance of new lines. Swinne has already referred to a connection of this kind between the periodic system and the X-ray spectra in connection with Kossel's theory. We can only expect a closer connection between the X-ray phenomena and the chemical properties of the elements, when the conditions on the surface of the atom are concerned. In agreement with what has been brought to light by investigations on absorption of X-rays in elements of lower atomic number, such as have been performed in recent years in the physical laboratory at Lund, we understand immediately that the position and eventual structure of the absorption edges will to a certain degree depend upon the physical and chemical conditions under which the element investigated exists, while such a dependence does not appear in the characteristic emission lines.

If we attempt to obtain a more detailed explanation of the experimental observations, we meet the question of the influence of the presence of the other electrons in the atom upon the firmness of the binding of an electron in a given type of orbit. This influence will, as we at once see, be least for the inner parts of the atom, where for each electron the attraction of the nucleus is large in proportion to the repulsion of the other electrons. It should also be recalled, that while the relative influence of the presence of the other electrons upon the firmness of the binding will decrease with increasing charge of the nucleus, the effect of the variation in the mass of the electron with the velocity upon the firmness of the binding will increase strongly. This may be seen from Sommerfeld's formula (11). While we obtain a fairly good agreement for the levels corresponding to the removal of one of the innermost electrons in the atom by using the simple formula (11), it is, however, already necessary to take the influence of the other electrons into consideration in making an approximate calculation of the levels corresponding to a removal of an electron from one of the outer groups in the atom. Just this circumstance offers us, however, a possibility of obtaining information about the configurations of the electrons in the interior of the atoms from the X-ray spectra. Numerous investigations have been directed at this question both by Sommerfeld and his pupils and by Debye, Vegard and others. It may also be remarked that de Broglie and Dauvillier in a recent paper have thought it possible to find support in the experimental material for certain assumptions about the numbers of electrons in the groups of the atom to which Dauvillier had been led by considerations about the periodic system similar to those proposed by Langmuir and Ladenburg. In calculations made in connection with these investigations it is assumed that the electrons in the various groups move in separate concentric regions of the atom, so that the effect of the presence of the electrons in inner groups upon the motion of the electrons in outer groups as a first approximation may be expected to consist in a simple screening of the nucleus. On our view, however, the conditions are essentially different, since for the calculation of the firmness of the binding of the electrons it is necessary to take into consideration that the electrons in the more lightly bound groups in general during a certain fraction of their revolution will penetrate into the region of the orbits of electrons in the more firmly bound groups. On account of this fact, many examples of which we saw in the series spectra, we cannot expect to give an account of the firmness of the binding of the separate electrons, simply by means of a "screening correction" consisting in the subtraction of a constant quantity from the value for N in such formulae as (5) and (11). Furthermore in the calculation of the work corresponding to the energy levels we must take account not only of the interaction between, the electrons in the normal state of the atom, but also of the changes in the configuration and interaction of the remaining electrons, which establish themselves automatically without emission of radiation during the removal of the electron. Even though such calculations have not yet been made very accurately, a preliminary investigation has already shown that it is possible approximately to account for the experimental results.

Classification of X-ray spectra. Independently of a definite view of atomic structure it has been possible by means of a formal application of Kossel's and Sommerfeld's theories to disentangle the large amount of experimental material on X-ray spectra. This material is drawn mainly from the accurate measurements of Siegbahn and his collaborators. From this disentanglement of the experimental observations, in which besides Sommerfeld and his students especially Smekal and Coster have taken part, we have obtained a nearly complete classification of the energy levels corresponding to the X-ray spectra. These levels are formally referred to types of orbits characterized by two quantum numbers n and k, and certain definite rules for the possibilities of combination between the various levels have also been found. In this way a number of results of great interest for the further elucidation of the origin of the X-ray spectra have been attained. First it has not only been possible to find levels, which within certain limits correspond to all possible pairs of numbers for n and k, but it has been found that in general to each such pair more than one level must be assigned. This result, which at first may appear very surprising, upon further consideration can be given a simple interpretation. We must remember that the levels depend not only upon the constitution of the atom in the normal state, but also upon the configurations which appear after the removal of one of the inner electrons and which in contrast to the normal state do not possess a uniquely completed character. If we thus consider a process in which one of the electrons in a group (subgroup) is removed we must be prepared to find that after the process the orbits of the remaining electrons in this group may be orientated in more than one way in relation to one another, and still fulfil the conditions required of the stationary states by the quantum theory. Such a view of the "complexity" of the levels, as further consideration shows, just accounts for the manner in which the energy difference of the two levels varies with the atomic number. Without attempting to develop a more detailed picture of atomic structure, Smekal has already discussed the possibility of accounting for the multiplicity of levels. Besides referring to the possibility that the separate electrons in the principal groups do not move in equivalent orbits, Smekal suggests the introduction of three quantum numbers for the description of the various groups, but does not further indicate to what extent these quantum numbers shall be regarded as characterizing a complexity in the structure of the groups in the normal state itself or on the contrary characterizing the incompleted groups which appear when an electron is removed.

It will be seen that the complexity of the X-ray levels exhibits a close analogy with the explanation of the complexity of the terms of the series spectra. There exists, however, this difference between the complex structure of the X-ray spectra and the complex structure of the lines in the series spectra, that in the X-ray spectra there occur not only combinations between spectral terms, for which k varies by unity, but also between terms corresponding to the same value of k. This may be assumed to be due to the fact, that in the X-ray spectra in contrast to the series spectra we have to do with transitions between stationary states where, both before and after the transition, the electron concerned takes

Niton

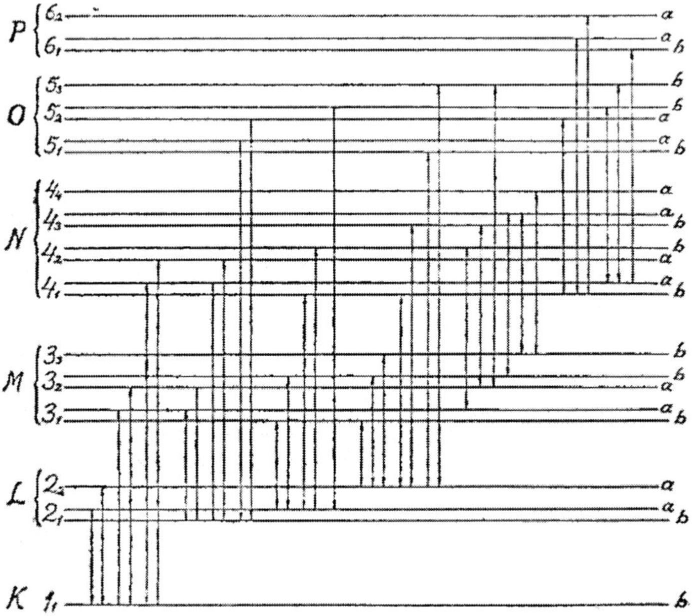

Fig. 5.

part in an intimate interaction with other electrons in orbits with the same principal quantum number. Even though this interaction may be assumed to be of such a nature that the harmonic components which would appear in the motion of an electron in the absence of the others will in general also appear in the resulting moment of the atom, we must expect that the interaction between the electrons will give rise to the appearance in this moment of new types of harmonic components.

It may be of interest to insert here a few words about a new paper of Coster which appeared after this address was given, and in which he has succeeded in obtaining an extended and detailed connection between the X-ray spectra and the ideas of atomic structure given in this essay. The classification mentioned above was based on measurements of the spectra of the heaviest elements, and the results in their complete form, which were principally due to independent work of Coster and Wentzel, may be represented by the diagram in fig. 5, which refers to elements in the neighbourhood of niton. The vertical arrows represent the

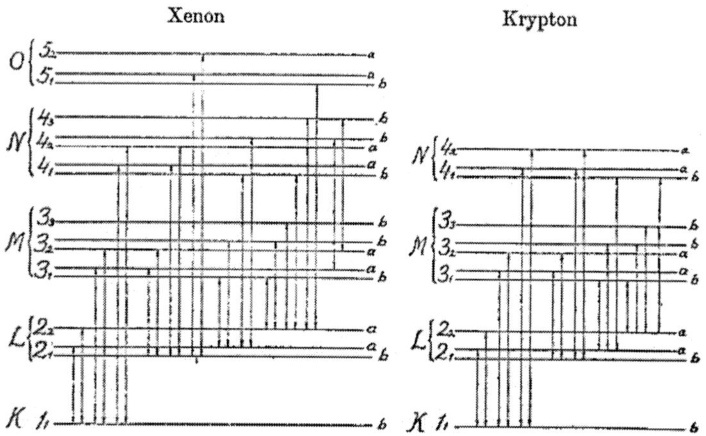

Fig. 6.

observed lines arising from combinations between the different energy levels which are represented by horizontal lines. In each group the levels are arranged in the same succession as their energy values, but their distances do not give a quantitative picture of the actual energy-differences, since this would require a much larger figure. The numbers n_k attached to the different levels indicate the type of the corresponding orbit. The letters a and b refer to the rules of combination which I mentioned. According to these rules the possibility of combination is limited (1) by the exclusion of combinations, for which k changes by more than one unit, (2) by the condition that only combinations between an a- and a b-level can take place. The latter rule was given in this form by Coster; Wentzel formulated it in a somewhat different way by the formal introduction of a third quantum number. In his new paper Coster has established a similar classification for the lighter elements. For the elements in the neighbourhood of xenon and krypton he has obtained results illustrated by the diagrams given in fig. 6. Just as in fig. 5 the levels correspond exactly to those types of orbits which, as seen from the table on page 170, according to the theory will be present in the atoms of these elements. In xenon several of the levels present in niton have disappeared, and in krypton still more levels have fallen away. Coster has also investigated in which elements these particular levels appear for the last time, when passing from higher to lower atomic number. His results concerning this point confirm in detail the predictions of the theory. Further he proves that the change in the firmness of binding of the electrons in the outer groups in the elements of the family of the rare earths shows a dependence on the atomic number which strongly supports the assumption that in these elements a completion of an inner group of 4-quanta orbits takes place. For details the reader is referred to Coster's paper in the *Philosophical Magazine*. Another important contribution to our systematic knowledge of the X-ray spectra is contained in a recent paper by Wentzel. He shows that various lines, which find no place in the classification hitherto considered, can be ascribed in a natural manner to processes of reorganization, initiated by the removal of more than one electron from the atom; these lines are therefore in a certain sense analogous to the enhanced lines in the optical spectra.

CONCLUSION

Before bringing this address to a close I wish once more to emphasize the complete analogy in the application of the quantum theory to the stability of the atom, used in explaining two so different phenomena as the periodic system and X-ray spectra. This point is of the greatest importance in judging the reality of the theory, since the justification for employing considerations, relating to the formation of atoms by successive capture of electrons, as a guiding principle for the investigation of atomic structure might appear doubtful if such considerations could not be brought into natural agreement with views on the reorganization of the atom after a disturbance in the normal electronic arrangement. Even though a certain inner consistency in this view of atomic structure will be recognized, it is, however, hardly necessary for me to emphasize the incomplete character of the theory, not only as regards the elaboration of details, but also so far as the foundation of the general points of view is concerned. There seems, however, to be no other way of advance in atomic problems than that which hitherto has been followed, namely to let the work in these two directions go hand in hand.